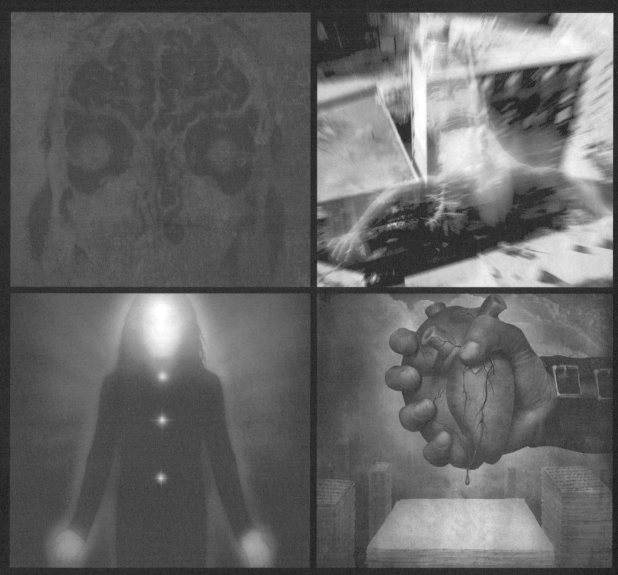

Exclusive Distributors:
Music Sales Limited
Distribution Centre, Newmarket Road, Bury St. Edmunds,
Suffolk IP33 3YB, England.
Music Sales Pty Limited
120 Rothschild Avenue, Rosebury, NSW 2018, Australia.

Order No. AM979110
ISBN 1-84449-334-2
This book © Copyright 2003 by Wise Publications.

Printed in the USA.

www.musicsales.com

Transcribed by Steve Gorenberg

Album design by Metallica
Cover illustrations by Pushead
Album production design by Brad Klausen
Photography by Anton Corbijn
St. Anger illustrations by Matt Mahurin
James image by Matt Mahurin
Lars image by Forhelvede Productions
Kirk image by Matt Mahurin
Robert image by Pascal Brun & Comenius Röthlisberger
   (Team Switzerland)
Management by Q Prime Inc.

Wise Publications
part of The Music Sales Group
London/New York/Paris/Sydney/Copenhagen/Berlin/Madrid/Tokyo

INTRODUCTION

When you're able to brandish the kind of musical firepower that Metallica has unleashed for more than two decades—ten uncompromising albums, marking an unprecedented reign as *the greatest* hard rock band in history—you learn a thing or two about where to aim. But curiously enough, the making of their first studio album since 1997's *ReLoad*, the primal, raptorial, *St. Anger*, found Metallica not behind the turrets this time, but in the firing line itself.

The trials and tribulations leading up to *St. Anger* are well documented. The fissures in what the band members themselves describe as the well-oiled "Metallica machine" were beginning to show. Bassist Jason Newsted's nebulous exit from the group. James Hetfield's voluntary sojourn into rehab and much-longed-for sobriety. Public squabbles over the illegal downloading quagmire. All of these issues revealed the kind of seismic fault lines that even the Metallica juggernaut could not navigate—could not negotiate away.

At stake? Nothing less than the very existence of the band itself. Metallica's three principals,

James Hetfield, Lars Ulrich, and Kirk Hammett, along with their frequent producer/collaborator Bob Rock, found themselves at the kind of crossroads worthy of the themes in many a Metallica song—the kind of foreboding scenario Ulrich and Hetfield could write in their sleep.

The irony was, if this was Metallica's oft-predicted *meltdown*, each member would have to face it in his own way. And from the inside out this time, without the Metallica heat shield to fend off all the bullshit that tends to calcify when you're a member of the most exclusive rock club in the world for 20-odd years. With James on an indefinite hiatus, the group admitted to becoming "professional speculators" themselves as to whether Metallica was headed for a rebirth or would wither away on life support.

"It has been a very interesting three years," Lars Ulrich begins, with atypical understatement. "A very different three years for us. Difficult, awkward. It's been a ride that's taken us to places inside ourselves, inside the band, inside the potential of human beings and the

music and everything else that we could n[o]t imagine existed. But if you asked me then, [I] would say for the first time in my life wit[h] Metallica, I was starting to prepare myself tha[t] maybe the ride was over."

If it sounds like the tenets of a Herculea[n] struggle, who else but Metallica to apply for th[e] job. The result of the "ride" Lars refers to ca[n] indeed be found in the sweat and blood an[d] grooves of *St. Anger*. From the album'[s] crushing title song and its burnished heaps o[f] magnified guitar and drums, to the colossa[l] time and tempo changes of "Frantic," to the chugging slabs and staccato exchanges of the exalting confessional "My World," Metallica has once again, in the boldest strokes imaginable, made music its most viable currency.

The three band members, who gingerly refer t[o] themselves as brothers—and mean it— emerged from the other side of their journey with their musical compass intact. *St. Anger* i[s] an album that invariably will draw comparison[s] to their best work, to Metallica's halcyon days most notably their classic 1983 opus *Kill 'Em All*, and 1986's *Master of Puppets*. Monu mental in scope, the new album also recalls— by its sheer willfulness—the group's 15-million selling masterpiece known as the Black album. But this is clearly a work that couldn'[t] have been made 20 years ago. Not even [a] decade ago, though it fits the Metallica canor like a glove.

According to producer Rock (the Black album was his first collaboration with Metallica) *St. Anger* completes the circular creative cycle tha[t] only the greatest artists are able to sustain "It's been my experience that only the big artists know how to achieve a goal in their career, like Metallica did with the Black album Fewer still could have gone through what the[y] experienced with all their personal journeys throw away the rulebook, and try to capture the soul and truth of Metallica again. I think the rea[l] vision was to almost take them back to where they were first getting together, when three o[r] four guys get together and say: This is the kind of music we like; let's write some songs."

For James, whose own personal quest may have been the tipping point for Metallica's in spirational sea change, the album was ar

Kirk Hammett   Robert Trujillo   Lars Ulrich   James Hetfield

important step in their evolution not just as band members, but also as friends. "The early days of Metallica were about brotherhood, just survival mode, relying on each other and stuff. As the machine got bigger, you tend to forget about the friendship part and start worrying about where the machine is going. You get a little more protective, a little more isolated. Certain factors ignited the need to look inward again and just get to be friends. Now we're stronger than ever because we know what we're doing and we have experience on our side too."

Part of the familial equation the group had to deal with was the departure of Newsted and the search for a new bassist. Enter Rob Trujillo. A former member of Suicidal Tendencies and one of the masterminds behind the '90s cult band Infectious Grooves, the accomplished bassist has also played with none other than Ozzy Osbourne.

All three band members immediately hit it off with the respected Trujillo, and the hole in Metallica's musical armor was filled. Trujillo came aboard too late to appear on *St. Anger*. The band members did not seem to be in any rush to hire a bass player. Bob Rock, in addition to being the co-producer and co-songwriter on St. Anger, was considered the fourth member of the band. Bob even filled in (quite masterfully) at a few live events with the guys. But, as Metallica guitarist Kirk Hammett points out, Trujillo's chemistry with the band is undeniable. "From the first rehearsal Rob was just mind-blowing, because he had such a huge sound and he pulled with his fingers, which is very reminiscent of Cliff Burton, and we really liked that sound. He delivered on all fronts. He had a big sound and on top of that he's really a great, solid guy." Adds James: "He pounds. The power that comes through his fingers. He's a ball of energy and he's so calm and able and balanced. He's got great stuff to offer but his personality is just right. He's on fire, he's ready, he's plugged right into the strength of Metallica and helping it shine."

Another aspect of Metallica's rejuvenated approach on this album is Hammett's joining in on the lyric writing, territory previously exclusive to James and Lars. "At first I was like, I don't want anything to do with this; this is James' job. But Bob was very adamant. I

looked at James and I said, 'Well, how do I do this?' James said 'stream of consciousness.' I would scribble down some lines and James would single out the good ones. It was a great experience and I think it's all in line with the theme of the album, if there is an underlying theme, which is just being true to yourself and how important that is to the overall picture."

Which leads to what is sure to be another topic of discussion among Metallica-watchers when poring over the epic arrangements and knife-edged nuances of *St. Anger*. For a band that is in the throes of introspection, and in a larger sense, collective healing, they sure have laid down some motherfucking aggressive music. For hardcore fans who patiently waded through their all-covers release, 1998's *Garage Inc.*, a spry homage to the songs that shaped their early career, and the symphonic wanderlust of *S&M*, a stirring experiment that showcased Metallica with noted producer/writer/arranger Michael Kamen and the San Francisco Symphony, *St. Anger* is a thirst-quencher. But one that offers nothing but fire this time around.

Lars says there was no conscious effort to make this album louder or longer. "I think the great thing about Metallica is that we can pretty much chart where we want to chart. Playing other people's material (like on *Garage Inc.*) was something we talked about for years. It was the music the band was basically founded on. With the symphony stuff we got a call from Michael Kamen who wanted to do it and the band was excited by the challenge—something Metallica has always embraced. "But now that we are back playing the stuff that people think is the purest, it is the most natural, it is the most effortless. The other thing I think we're challenging here is the perception most people have that in order for things to be really, really, energetic, they can only come from negative energy. Metallica was fueled by negative energy for 20 years. Now we've spent a lot of time working on ourselves and on our relationships, and we've turned that around. Now Metallica is fueled by positive energy that has manifested itself so it sounds like the album we've made."

Case in point: "Some Kind of Monster," with its bristling, time bomb refrain, and yet, underneath, a hint of affirmation: "This is the voice of silence no more." You begin to understand the

complex dynamics required for a world-renowned construct like Metallica even to be able to conceive of an intensely personal triumph like *St. Anger*. For James the process obviously begins in a much quieter place than a recording studio. "It comes from us realizing the world doesn't revolve around Metallica. For me it began with "my name is James Hetfield." *St. Anger* means to me that now that we've found our serenity we're capable of making this monster of an album going full throttle all the time. Anger is an energy. It's a feeling. It's gotten a bad reputation, but it's what you do with it after that gives it its reputation. I could squeeze out sideways with rage and stuff the shit down, yet it can be such a source of strength. Metallica has always been about invading places where we don't belong. We just took down the barbed wire, that's all."

DISCOGRAPHY

Kill 'Em All	July 1983
Ride the Lightning	August 1984
Master of Puppets	February 1986
Garage Days Re-Revisited	August 1987
...And Justice for All	August 1988
Metallica	August 1991
Live Shit: Binge & Purge	December 1993
Load	June 1996
ReLoad	November 1997
Garage Inc.	November 1998
S&M	November 1999
St. Anger	June 2003

Metallica Web Site: www.metallica.com

Metallica Fan Club: www.metclub.com

Metallica Fan Club mailing address:

The Metallica Club
369-B Third St.
PMB #194
San Rafael, CA 94901

contents

FRANTIC

Words and Music by
James Hetfield, Lars Ulrich,
Kirk Hammett and Bob Rock

5 str. drop D tuning, down 1 step:
(low to high) A-C-G-C-F

Intro
Moderately fast Rock ♩ = 168

(Guitar)

D5

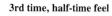

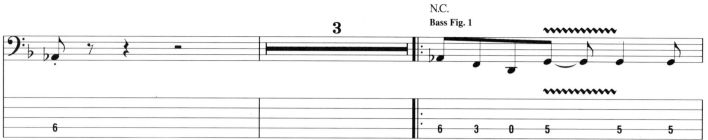

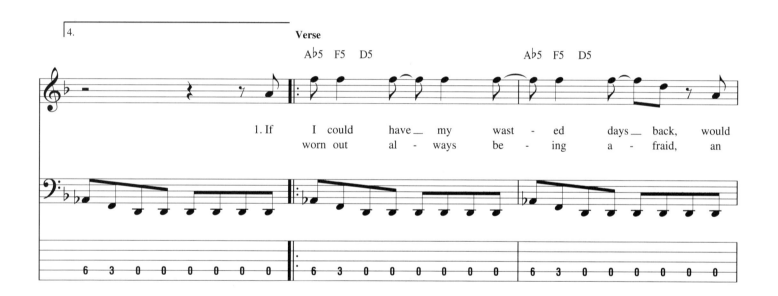

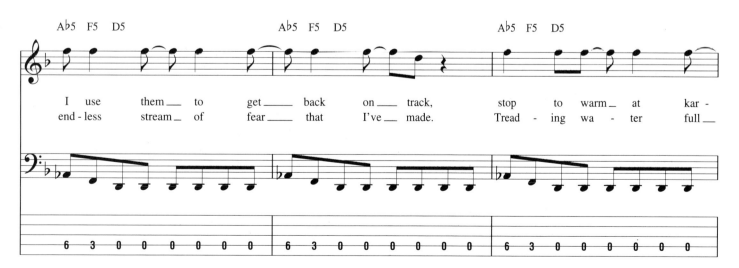

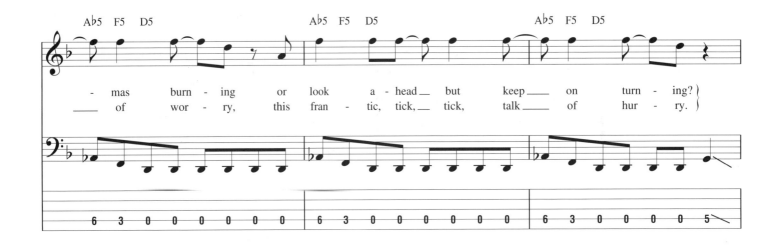

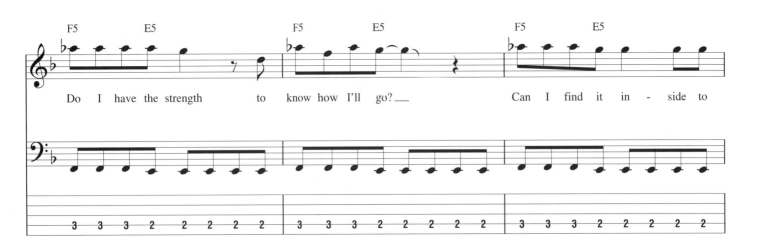

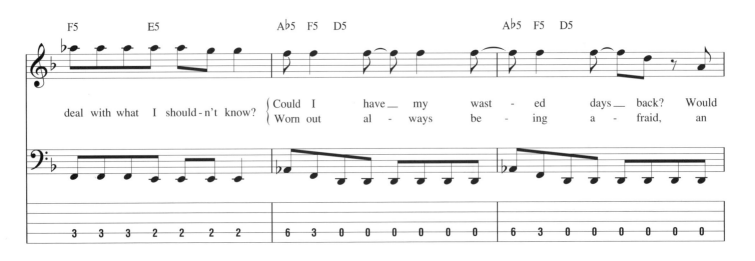

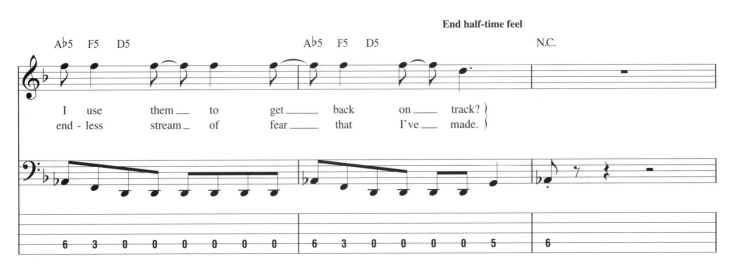

You live it or lie ____ it! You live it or lie ____ it! (You

live it or lie ____ it! You live it or lie ____ it! My life - style de -

D5

Bass Fig. 2

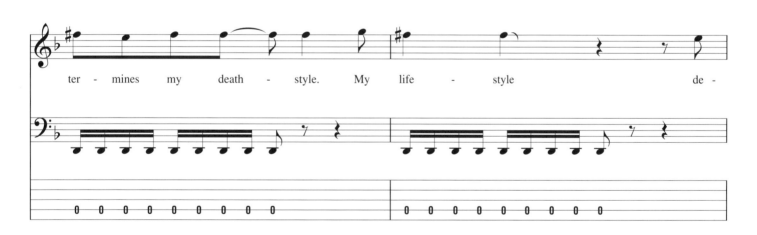

ter - mines my death - style. My life - style de -

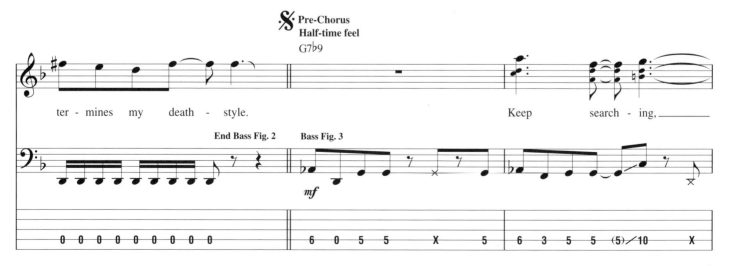

Pre-Chorus
Half-time feel

G7♭9

ter - mines my death - style. Keep search - ing, _____

End Bass Fig. 2   Bass Fig. 3

mf

9

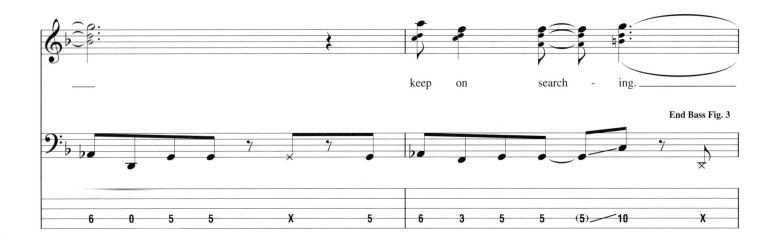

keep on search - ing.

End Bass Fig. 3

w/ Bass Fig. 3 (3 times)

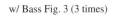

This search goes on,

1., 2. this search goes on.
3. on and on.

Keep search - ing,

keep on search - ing.

End half-time feel

This search goes on,

1. this search goes on.
2., 3. on and on.

Chorus

N.C.

Fran - tic, tick, tick, tick, tock.
Fran - tic, tick, tick,

Bass Fig. 4

10

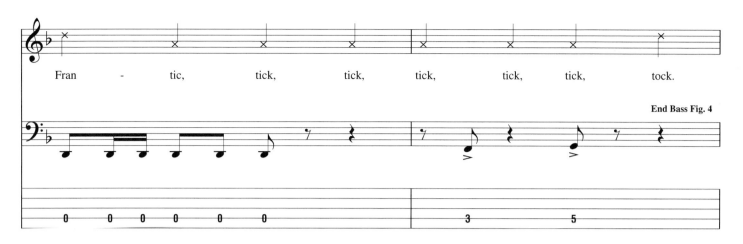

Fran - tic, tick, tick, tick, tick, tick, tock.

End Bass Fig. 4

To Coda ⊕

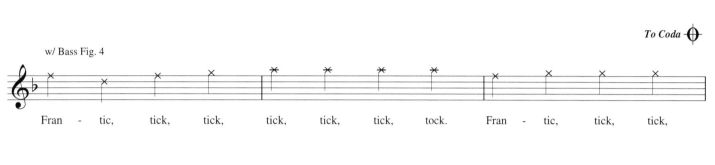

w/ Bass Fig. 4

Fran - tic, tick, tick, tick, tick, tick, tock. Fran - tic, tick, tick,

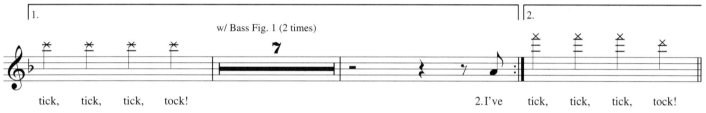

1.

w/ Bass Fig. 1 (2 times)

tick, tick, tick, tock!

2.

2.I've tick, tick, tick, tock!

Interlude

Half-time feel

4th time, end half-time feel

Play 4 times

N.C.

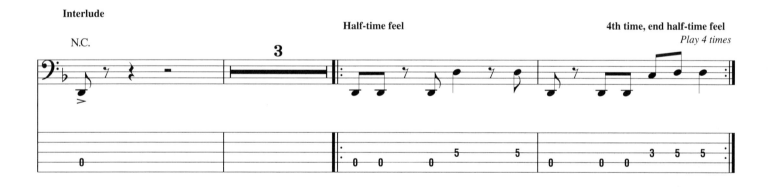

Bridge

N.C.

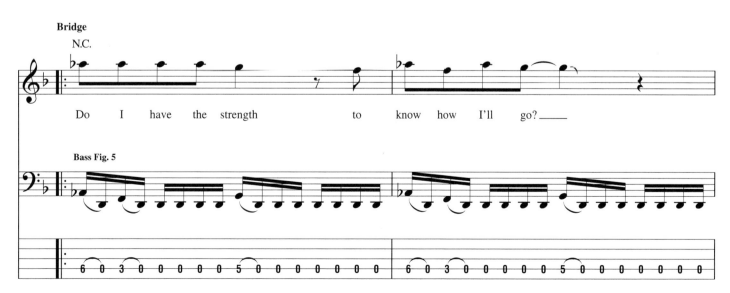

Do I have the strength to know how I'll go?____

Bass Fig. 5

Can I find it in - side to deal with what I should - n't know?_____

End Bass Fig. 5

1. w/ Bass Fig. 5   **3**   **2.** w/ Bass Fig. 2 (3 times)   **2**

_____   _____   Oh. _____ My

D5

life - style   de - ter - mines my death - style,   a   ris - ing tide   that
(Birth is pain.   Life is pain.

F5   **D5**

push - es to the oth - er side. My life - style   de - ter - mines my death - style, a
Death is pain.

D.S. al Coda   **Coda**
F5

ris - ing tide   that push - es to the oth - er side.   tick, tick, tick, tock!
It's all the same.)

Outro
Slower ♩ = 128

D5   *Play 4 times*

Play 3 times

ST. ANGER

Words and Music by
James Hetfield, Lars Ulrich,
Kirk Hammett and Bob Rock

5 str. drop D and A tuning, down 1 step:
(low to high) G-C-G-C-F

Intro
Fast Rock ♩ = 196

(Guitar)
N.C.

(Guitar)
N.C.

Drums

Play 3 times

Double-time feel

N.C.

Bass Fig. 1

Play 4 times
End Bass Fig. 1

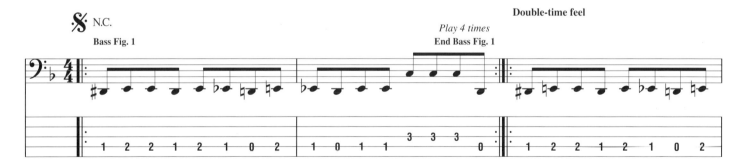

4th time, end double-time feel
Play 4 times

Bass Fig. 2

End Bass Fig. 2

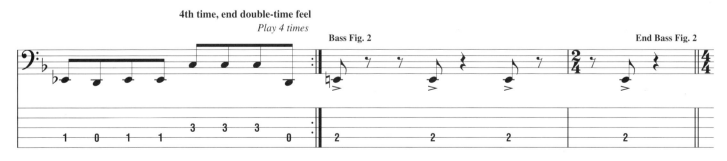

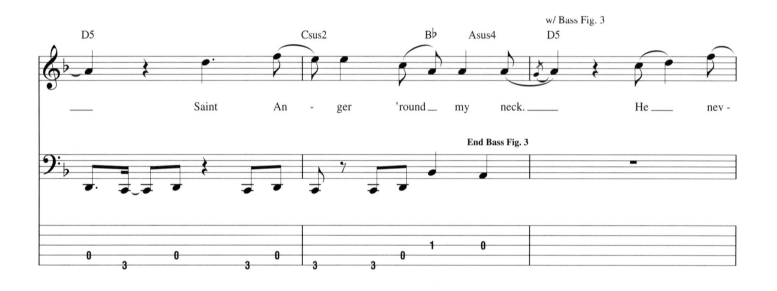

*Chord symbols reflect overall harmony.

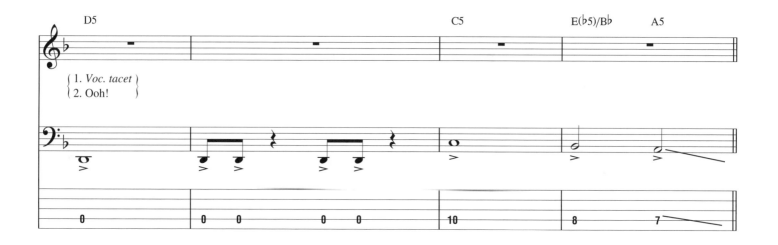

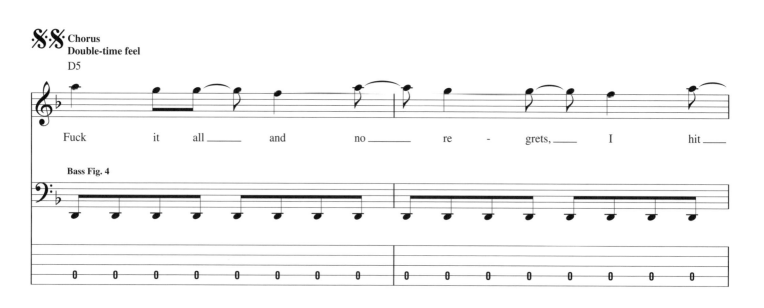

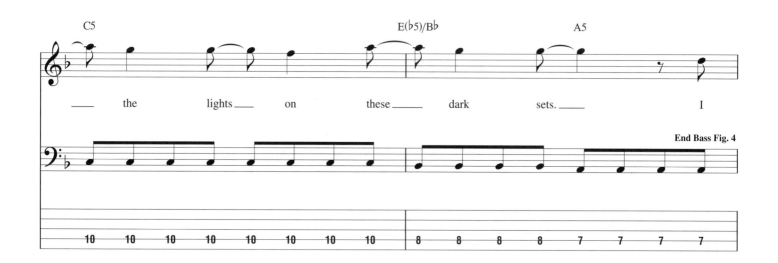

16

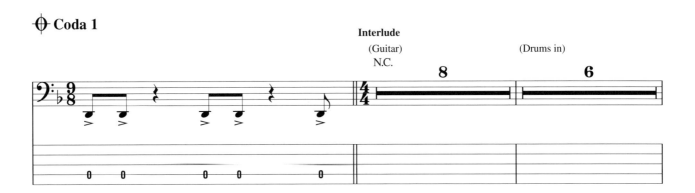

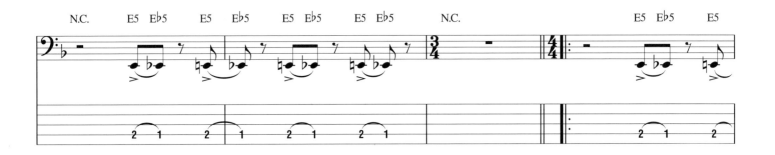

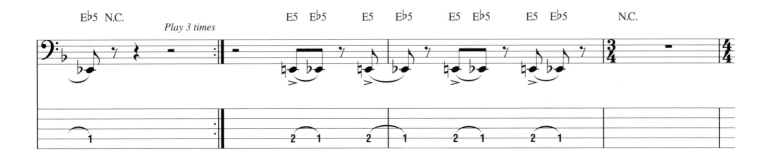

want   my   an - ger   just ___ for   me. ___

And   I   need   my   an - ger   not ___ to   con -

- trol. ___   Yeah, __ and   I   want   my

an - ger   to ___ be   me. ___

w/ Bass Fig. 1 (2 times)

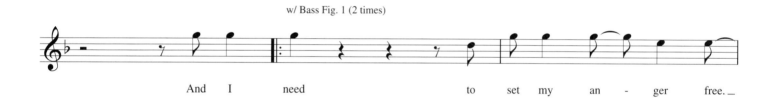

And   I   need   to   set   my   an - ger   free. __

w/ Bass Fig. 1 (4 times)

___   And   I   need   to

set   my   an - ger   free, ___ ah!   And   I

need   to   set   my   an - ger   free. ___

Interlude
Double-time feel
w/ Bass Fig. 1 (4 times)
N.C.

End double-time feel
w/ Bass Fig. 2

Set it free! _____

⊕ **Coda 2**

w/ Bass Fig. 4 (2 times)

E(♭5)/B♭   A5   D5

_____ I'm mad - ly in an - ger with you. ___

C5

___ I'm mad - ly in an - ger with you. ___

E(♭5)/B♭   A5   D5

_____ I'm mad - ly in an - ger with you. ___

End double-time feel

C5   E(♭5)/B♭   A5

_____ I'm mad - ly in an - ger with you. _____

D5

N.C.   D5

SOME KIND OF MONSTER

Words and Music by
James Hetfield, Lars Ulrich,
Kirk Hammett and Bob Rock

5 str. drop D tuning, down 1 step:
(low to high) A-C-G-C-F

Intro

Moderately slow Rock ♩ = 108

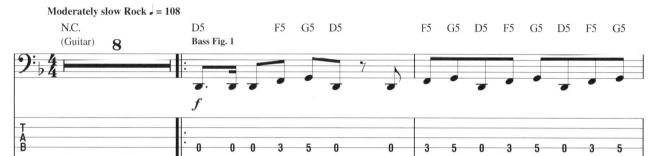

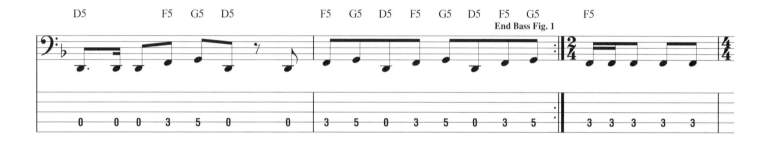

Double-time feel

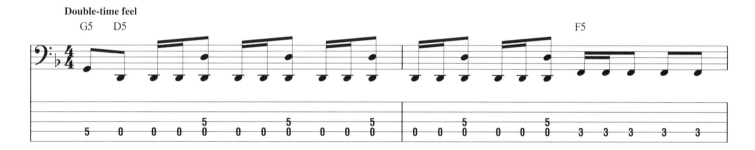

End double-time feel

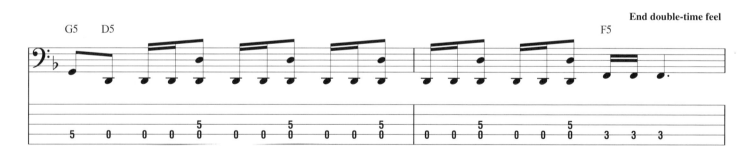

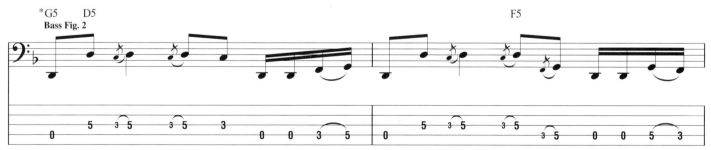

*Chord symbols refer to guitar.

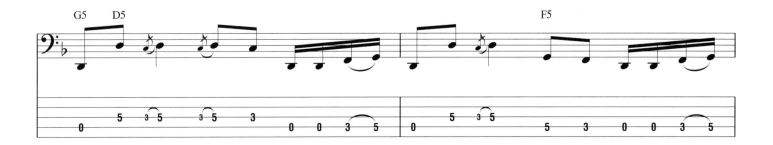

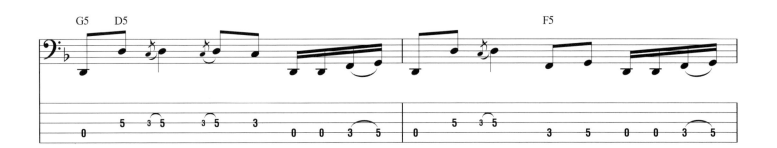

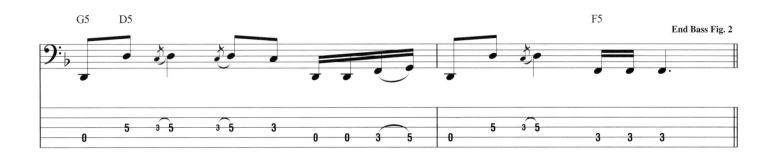

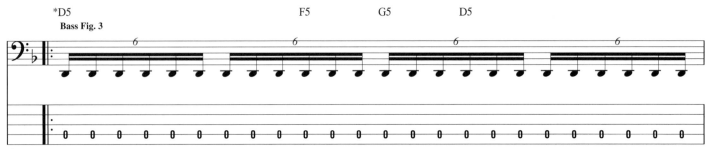

*Chord symbols refer to guitar (next 4 meas.)

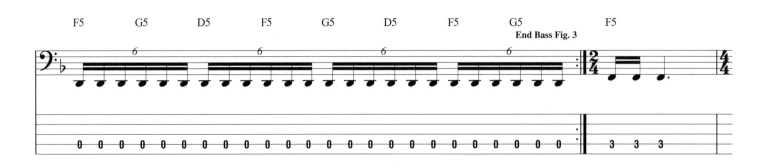

w/ Bass Fig. 2

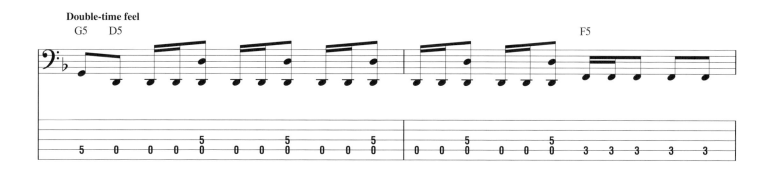

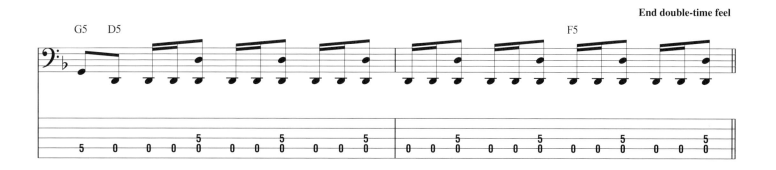

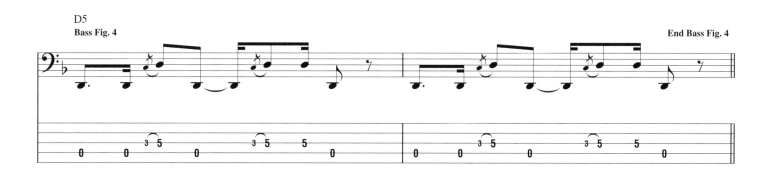

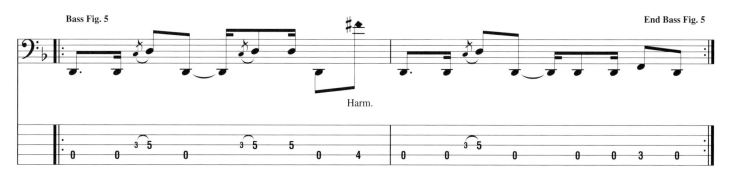

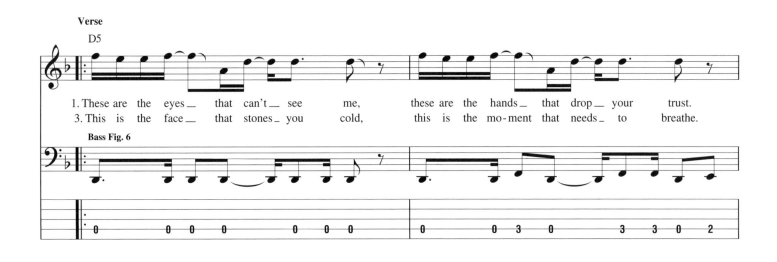

Verse

D5

1. These are the eyes_ that can't_ see me, these are the hands_ that drop_ your trust.
3. This is the face_ that stones_ you cold, this is the mo-ment that needs_ to breathe.

Bass Fig. 6

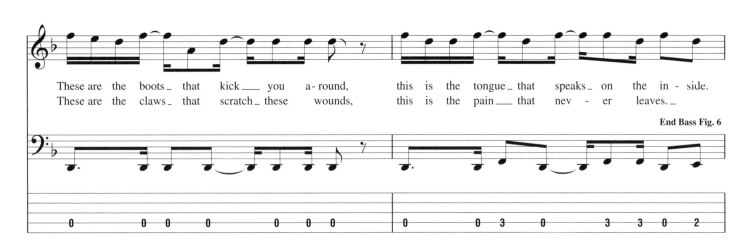

These are the boots_ that kick_ you a-round, this is the tongue_ that speaks_ on the in - side.
These are the claws_ that scratch_ these wounds, this is the pain__ that nev - er leaves._

End Bass Fig. 6

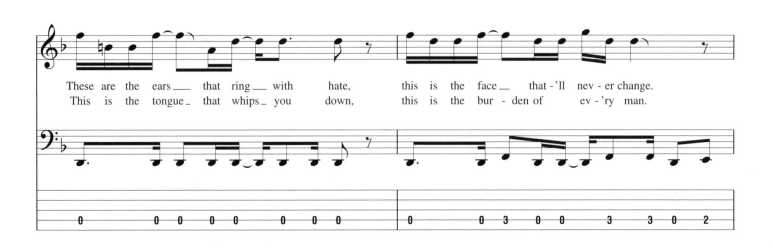

These are the ears__ that ring_ with hate, this is the face_ that -'ll nev - er change.
This is the tongue_ that whips_ you down, this is the bur - den of ev - 'ry man.

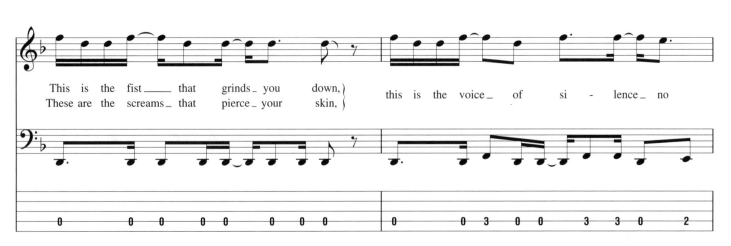

This is the fist____ that grinds_ you down,} this is the voice_ of si - lence_ no
These are the screams_ that pierce_ your skin,}

more.

N.C.

Interlude

Dm7

1. *Voc. tacet*
2. Yeah!   Yeah!   Yeah!   Yeah!   Yeah!   Yeah!

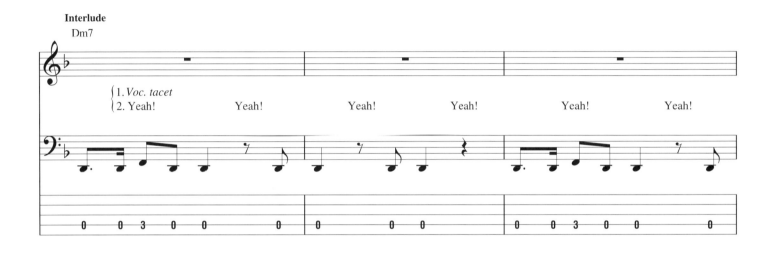

D5

Yeah!   Yeah!

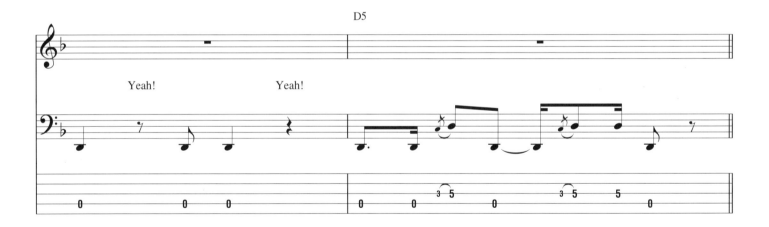

Verse

w/ Bass Fig. 6

D5

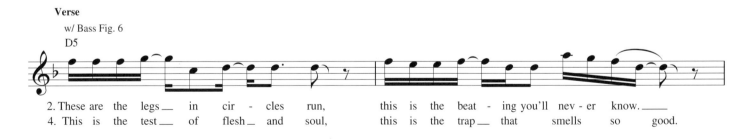

2. These are the legs __ in cir - cles run, this is the beat - ing you'll nev - er know. ____
4. This is the test __ of flesh __ and soul, this is the trap __ that smells so good.

These are the lips __ that taste __ no free - dom, this is the feel __ that's not __ so safe.
This is the flood __ that drains __ these eyes, these are the looks __ that chill __ to the bone.

This is the face ___ you'll nev - er change, this is the god ___ that ain't ___ so pure.
These are the fears ___ that swing o - ver head, these are the weights ___ that hold ___ you down.

This is the god ___ that is ___ not pure,
This is the end ___ that will nev - er end, } this is the voice ___ of si - lence ___ no

D5   D#5   E5

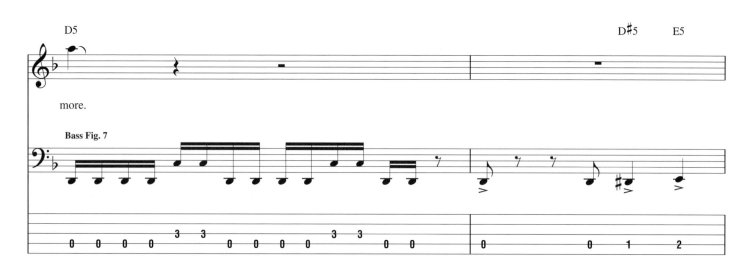

more.

Bass Fig. 7

D5   D#5   E5
                                                                     End Bass Fig. 7

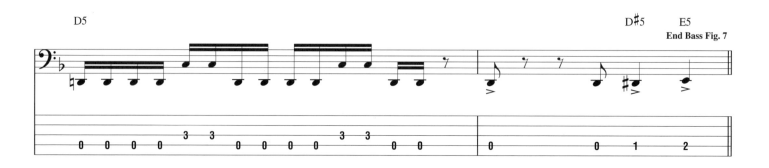

Pre-Chorus
N.C.

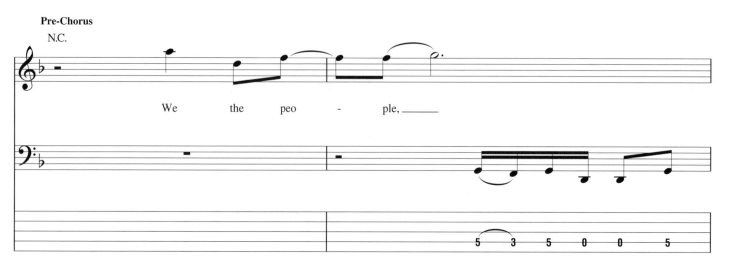

We the peo - ple, _____

This is the face___ that you___ hide from, this is the mask___ that comes___ un - done.___

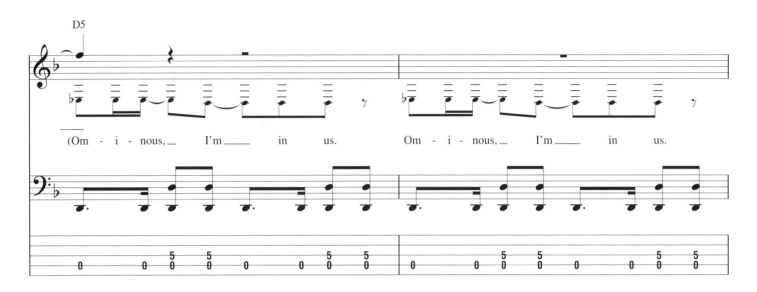

(Om - i - nous,___ I'm___ in us. Om - i - nous,___ I'm___ in us.

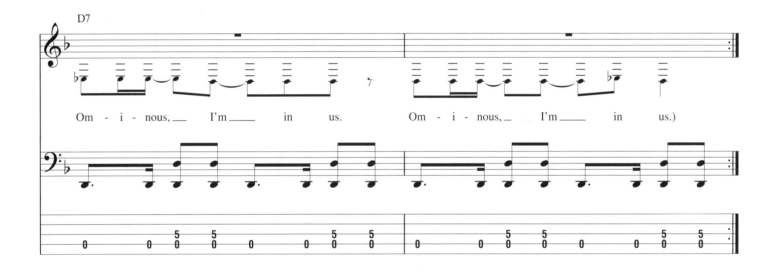

Om - i - nous,___ I'm___ in us. Om - i - nous,___ I'm___ in us.)

Interlude

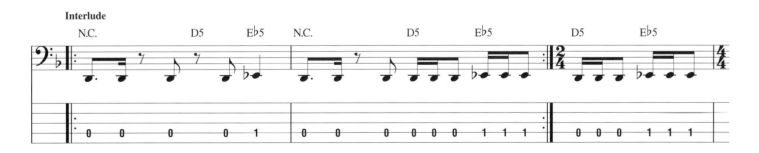

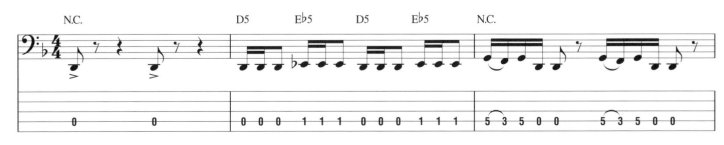

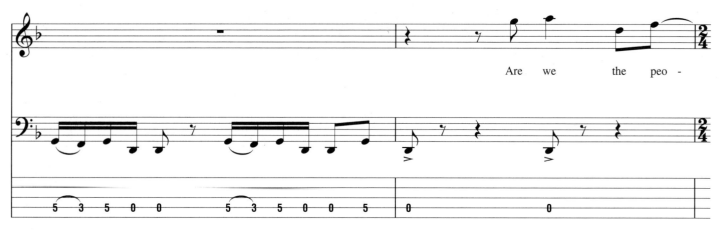

Are we the peo-

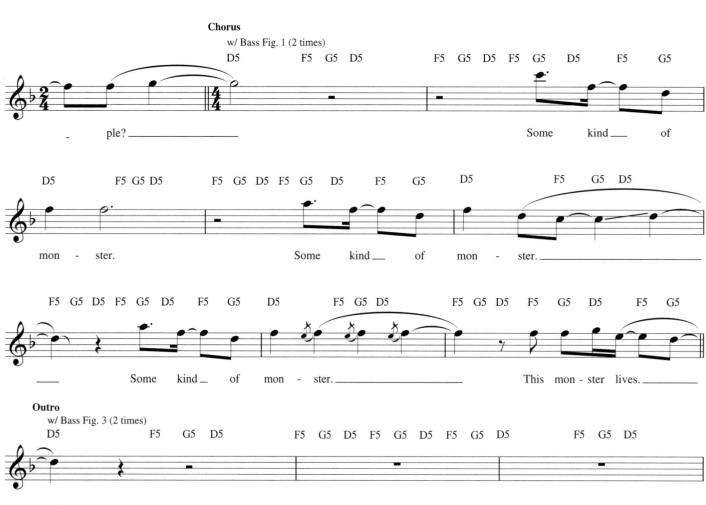

Chorus
w/ Bass Fig. 1 (2 times)

-ple? Some kind of

mon - ster. Some kind of mon - ster.

Some kind of mon - ster. This mon - ster lives.

Outro
w/ Bass Fig. 3 (2 times)

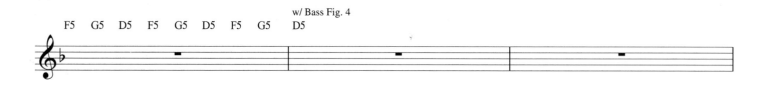

w/ Bass Fig. 4

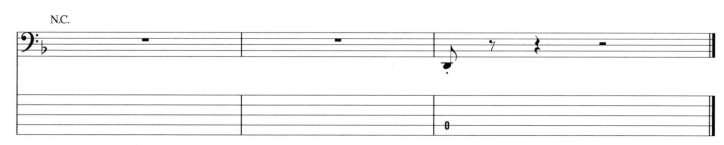

DIRTY WINDOW

Words and Music by
James Hetfield, Lars Ulrich,
Kirk Hammett and Bob Rock

5 str. drop D tuning, down 1/2 step:
(low to high) B♭-D♭-A♭-D♭-G♭

Intro
Moderate Rock ♩ = 136
(Guitar & drums)

*Chord symbols reflect implied harmony.

Double-time feel

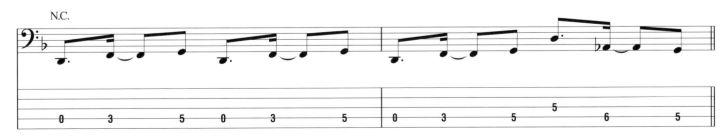

Verse

w/ Bass Fig. 1 (3 times)

N.C.

1., 2. I see my re - flec - tion in ___ the win - dow. ___

It ___ looks dif - f'rent, ___ so dif - f'rent ___ than what you see. ___
This win - dow, clean in - side, dirt - y on the out.

Pro - ject - ing judg - ment on the world. ___
I'm look - ing dif - fer - ent than me. ___

w/ Bass Fig. 2

End double-time feel

F6   F5   G5

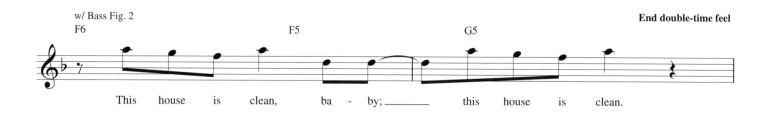

This house is clean, ba - by; ___ this house is clean.

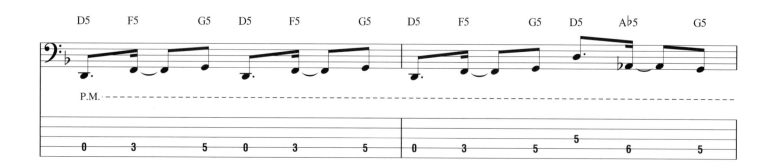

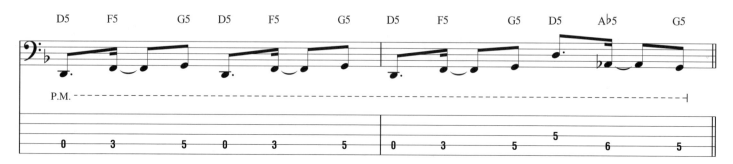

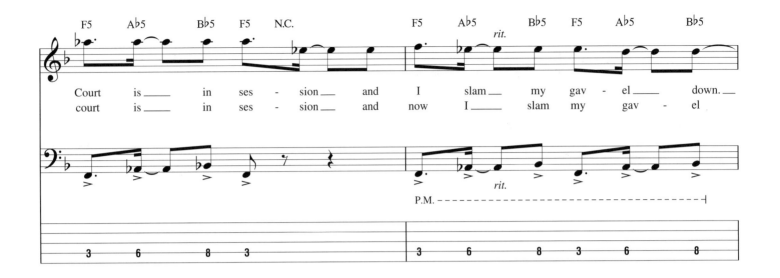

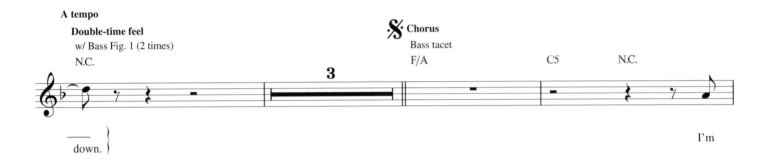

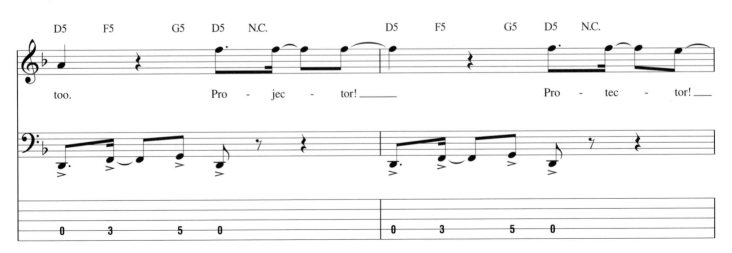

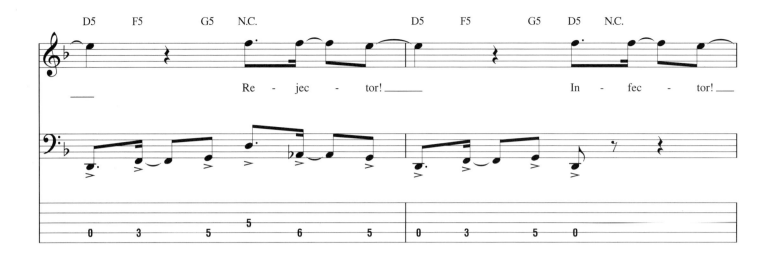

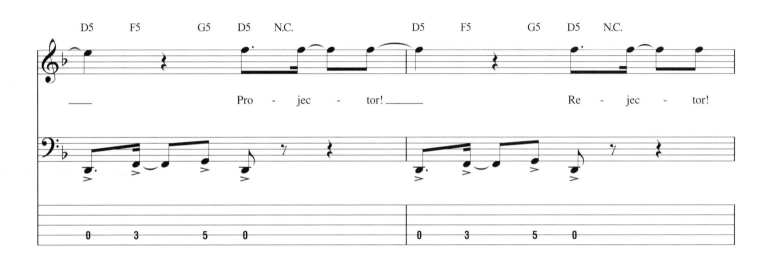

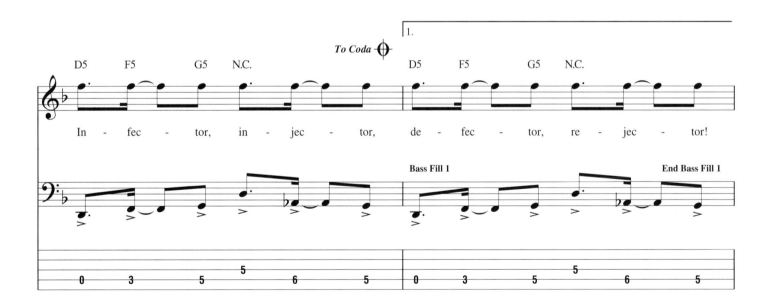

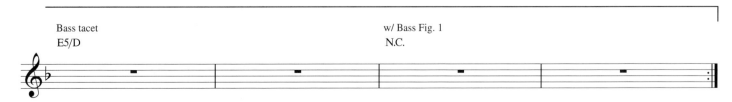

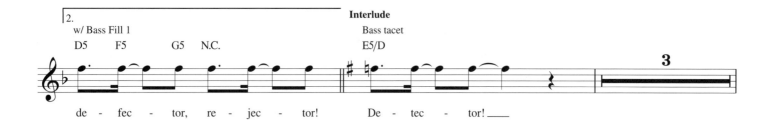

de - fec - tor, re - jec - tor! De - tec - tor! ____

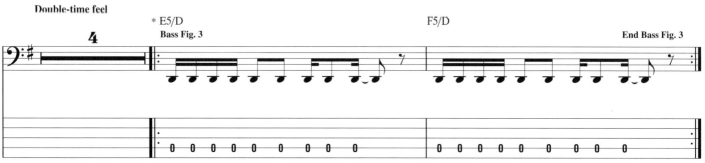

*Chord symbols reflect overall harmony.

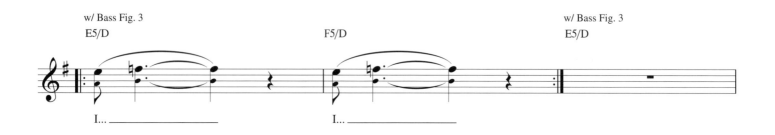

I... _____   I... _____

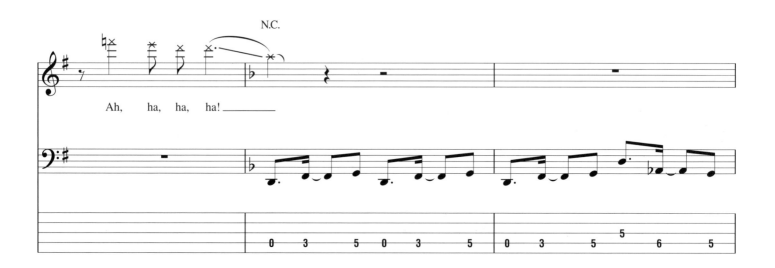

Ah,   ha,   ha,   ha! _____

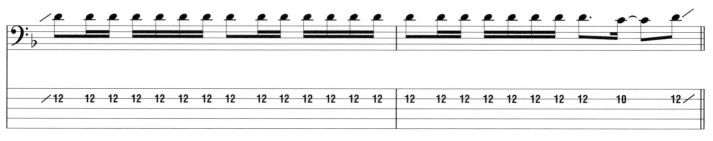

⊕ Coda

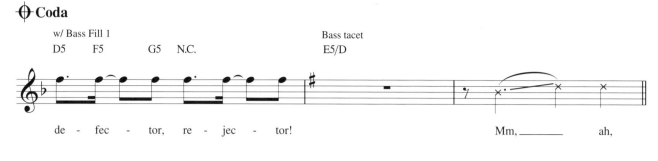

de - fec - tor, re - jec - tor!   Mm, _____ ah,

Interlude
Double-time feel

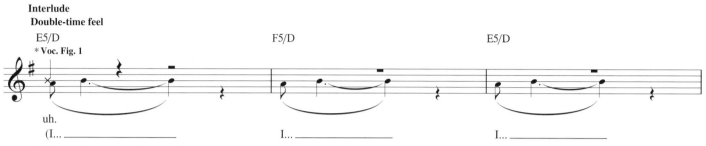

uh.
(I... _____   I... _____   I... _____

*Refers to downstemmed notes only.

Outro
Bkgd. Voc.: w/ Voc. Fig. 1 (4 times)

End Voc. Fig. 1

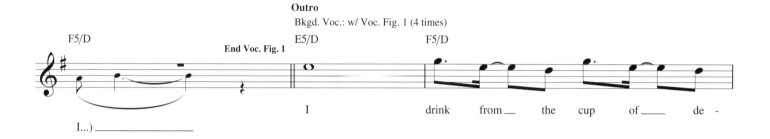

I... _____   I   drink   from __   the   cup   of __   de -

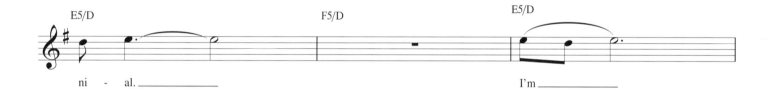

ni - al. _____   I'm _____

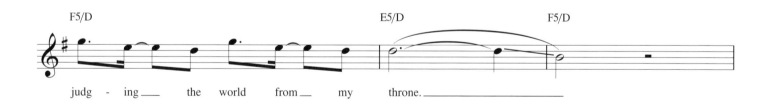

judg - ing __   the   world   from __   my   throne. _____

I   drink   from __ the   cup   of __   de -

37

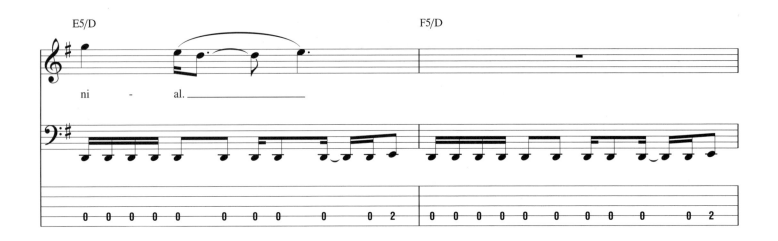

ni - al.

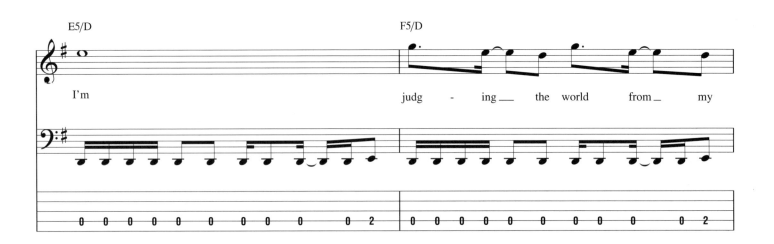

I'm judg - ing the world from my

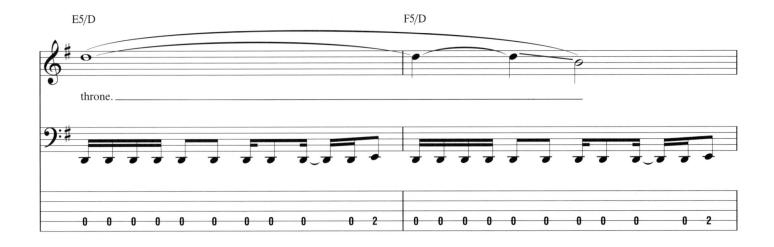

throne.

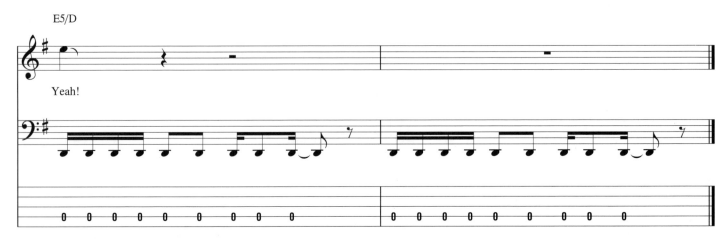

Yeah!

INVISIBLE KID

Words and Music by
James Hetfield, Lars Ulrich,
Kirk Hammett and Bob Rock

39

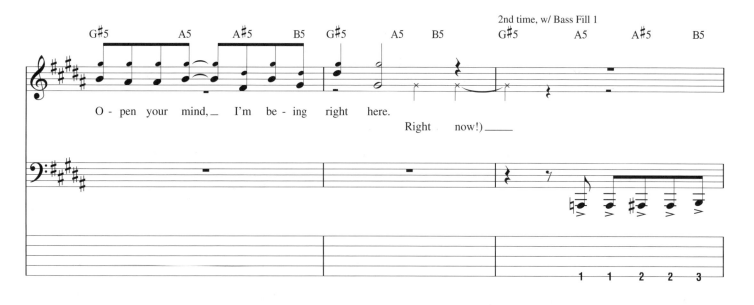

O - pen your mind,__ I'm be - ing right here.

Right now!)__

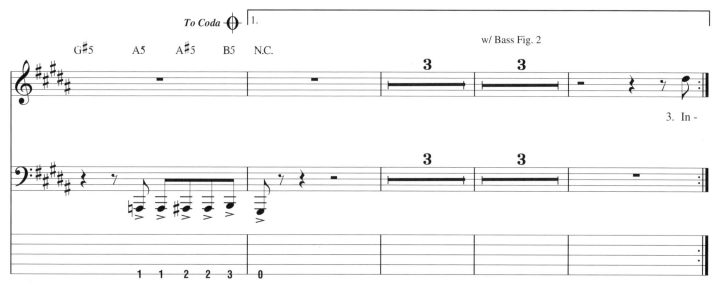

3. In -

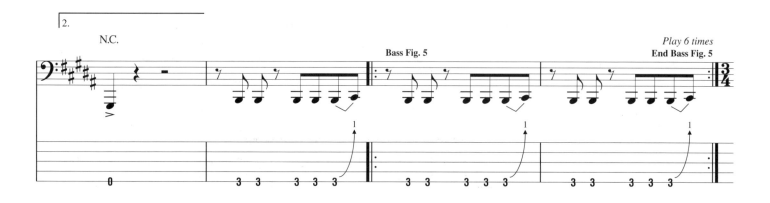

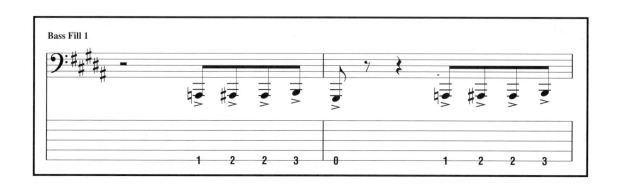

MY WORLD

Words and Music by
James Hetfield, Lars Ulrich,
Kirk Hammett and Bob Rock

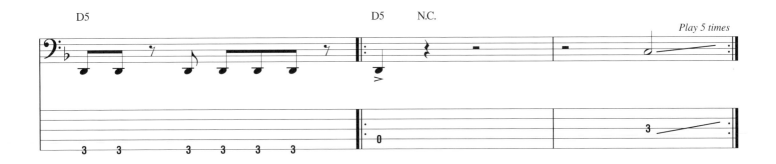

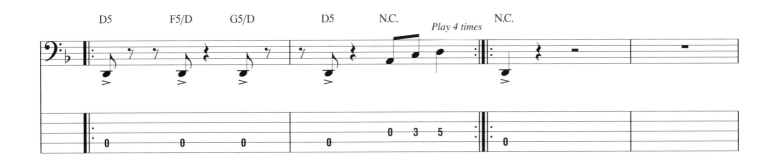

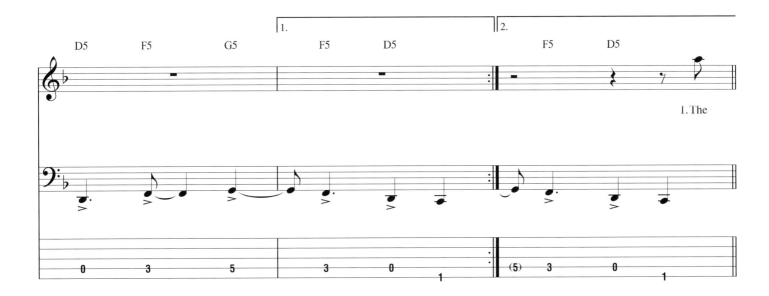

1. The

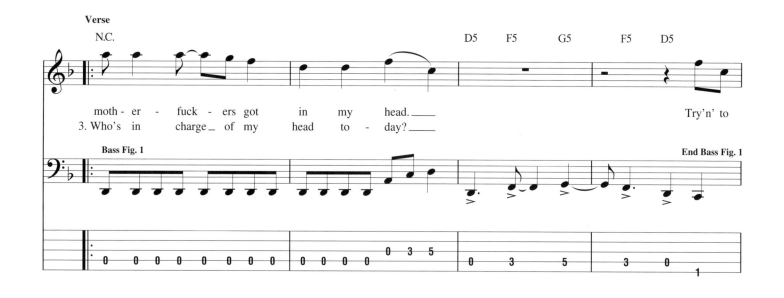

Verse

moth - er - fuck - ers got in my head. _____ Try 'n' to
3. Who's in charge_ of my head to - day? _____

make me some - one else _____ in - stead. It's
Danc - in' dev - ils in an - gels' way. It's

Half-time feel
w/ Bkgd. Voc. ad lib

my world now. _____ It's my world now. _____ It's
my time now. _____ It's my time now. _____ It's

End half-time feel

my world. _____ It's my world. _____
my time. _____ Yeah, it's my time. _____

48

Verse

w/ Bass Fig. 1 (4 times)

N.C.   D5   F5   G5   F5   D5

2. Ma - ma, why's it rain - ing in my room? ___

4. Look out, moth - er - fuck - ers, here I come. ___   I'm

N.C.   D5   F5   G5   F5   D5

Cheer up, boy; __ clouds will move on soon. __

gon - na make __ my head my home. __   The

N.C.   D5   F5   G5   F5   D5

Heav - y fog __ got me lost in - side. _____   I'm gon - na

sons - of - bitch - es try'n' to take my head. _____   Try'n' to

N.C.   D5   F5   G5   F5   D5

sit right back, __ en - joy ____ this ride. ____

make me some - one else ____ in - stead. ____   Ooh.

Chorus

D5   F5   G5

It's my world, __ you can't ____ have __ it. It's my world. __ It's my world. __

Bass Fig. 2   **End Bass Fig. 2**

```
0    3       5    5 5 5 5  5 5 5 5   5 5 5 5  5 5 5 5   5 5 5 5  5 5 5 5
```

w/ Bass Fig. 2 (2 times)

D5   F5   G5

It's my world, __ you can't ____ have it. It's my world. __ It's my world. __

D5   F5   G5

It's my world, __ you can't ____ have it. It's my world. __ It's my world. __

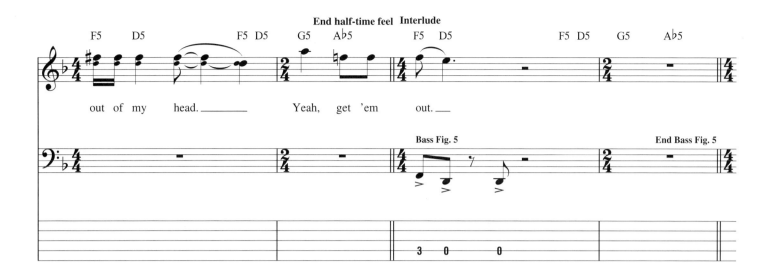

out of my head. _____ Yeah, get 'em out. ___

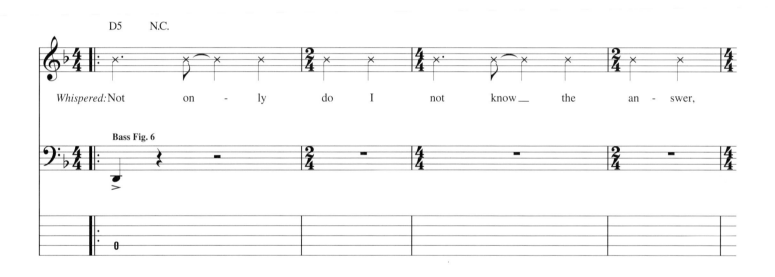

Whispered: Not on - ly do I not know ___ the an - swer,

I don't ___ e - ven know what the ___ ques - tion is.

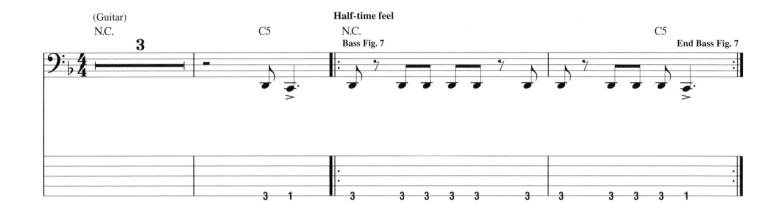

Bridge

w/ Bass Fig. 7 (14 times)

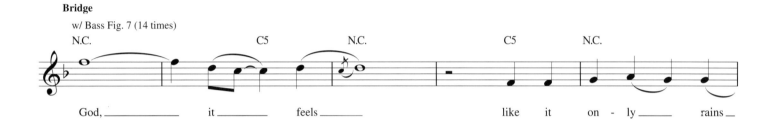

God, _____ it _____ feels _____ like it on - ly _____ rains _

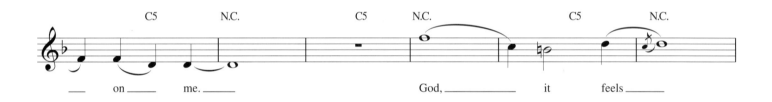

_ on _ me. _____ God, _____ it feels _____

like it on - ly _____ rains _____ on _ me.
(Like it on - ly _____ rains _____ on _ me.)

God, _____ it feels _____ like it on - ly _____ rains _

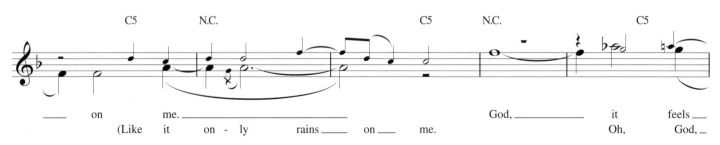

_ on me. _____ God, _____ it feels _
(Like it on - ly rains _____ on _ me. Oh, God, _

oh, God, oh, God. like it on - ly rains

End half-time feel Interlude

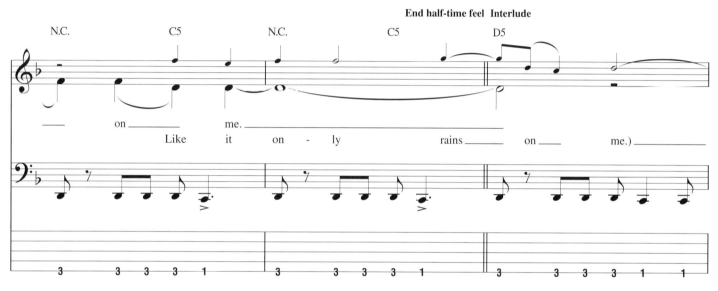

on me. Like it on - ly rains on me.)

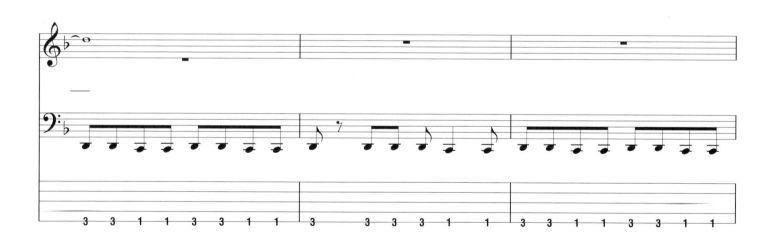

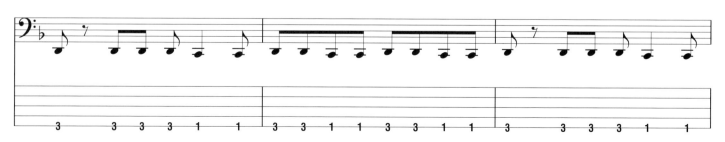

w/ Bass Fig. 6

Not on - ly do I not know ___ the an - swer,

I don't ___ e - ven know what the ___ ques - tion is.

w/ Bass Fig. 4 (2 times)

Half time feel

w/ Bass Fig. 3

w/ Bass Fig. 4 (2 times)

Suck - er!

w/ Bass Fig. 4 (4 times)

Out of my head, ___

out of my head. ___

Out of my head, ___ get 'em

End half-time feel Outro

out of my head. ___

Get 'em out!

Bass Fig. 8

54

End Bass Fig. 8

Play 4 times

w/ Bass Fig. 8 (4 times)

E - nough's   e - nough, __   e - nough's

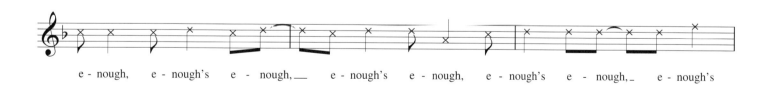

e - nough,   e - nough's   e - nough, __   e - nough's   e - nough,   e - nough's   e - nough, __   e - nough's

w/ Bass Fig. 3

A♭5   F5   D5   N.C.

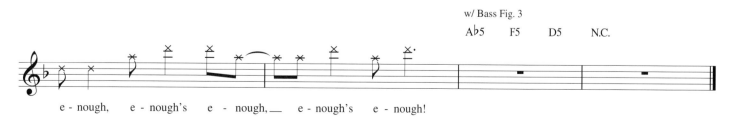

e - nough,   e - nough's   e - nough, __   e - nough's   e - nough!

SHOOT ME AGAIN

5 str. drop D tuning, down 1 step:
(low to high) A-C-G-C-F

Words and Music by
James Hetfield, Lars Ulrich,
Kirk Hammett and Bob Rock

Intro
Moderate Rock ♩ = 116

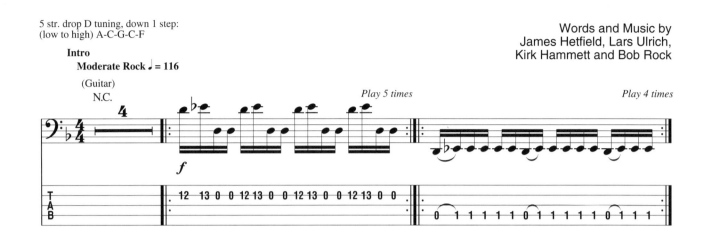

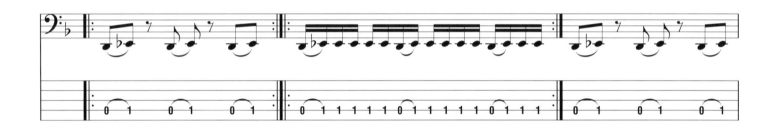

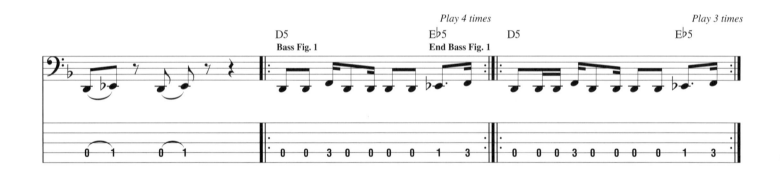

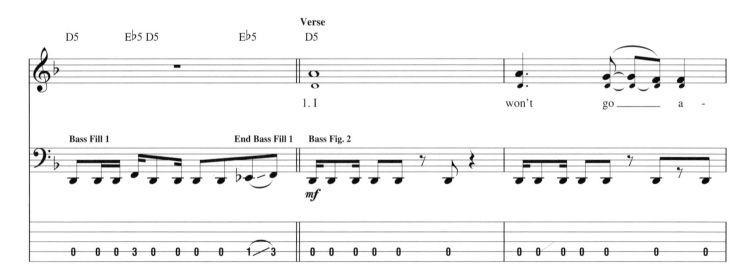

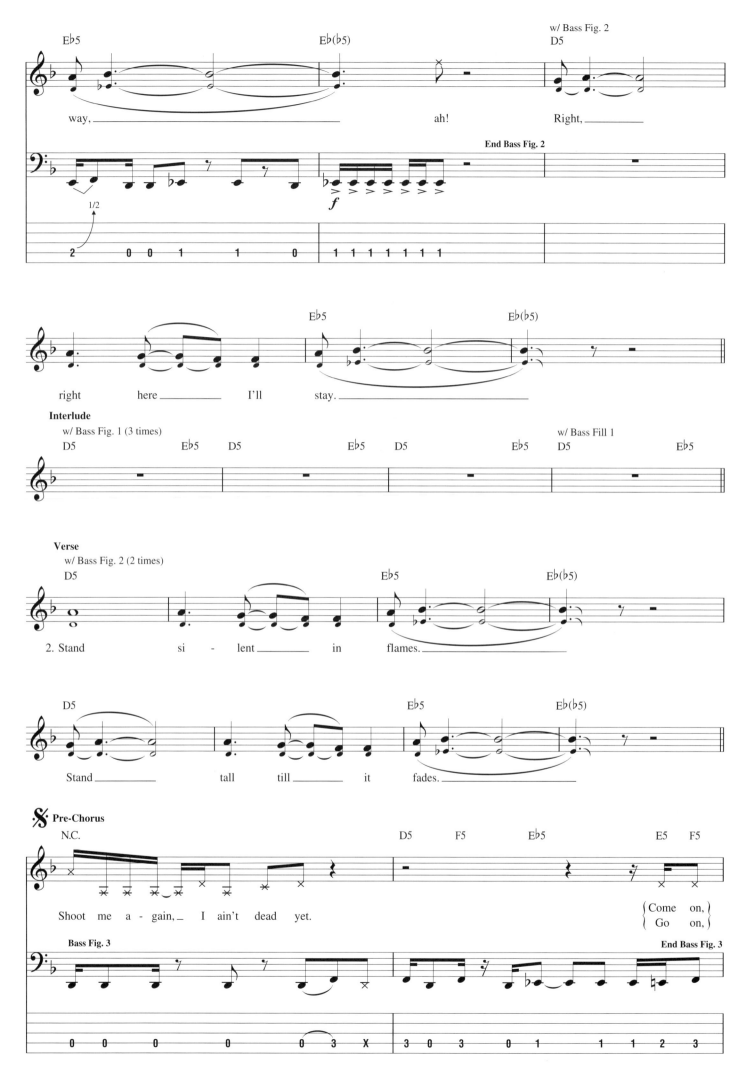

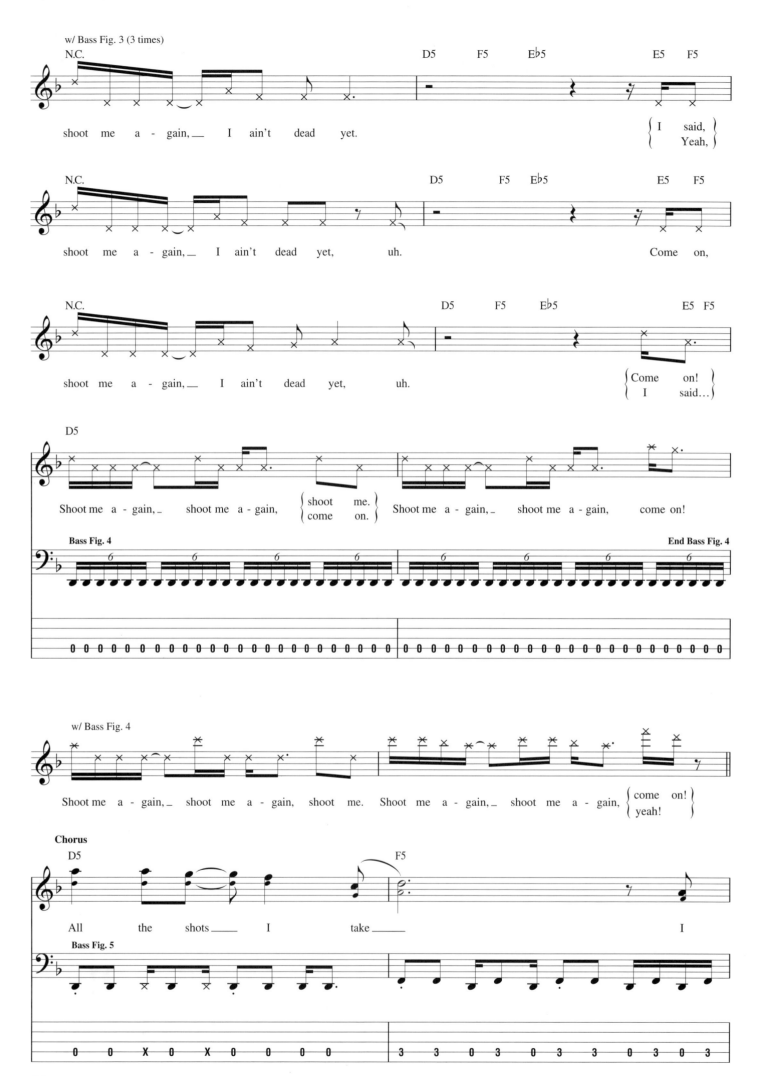

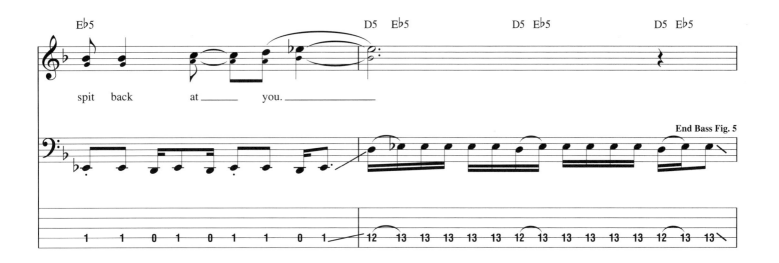

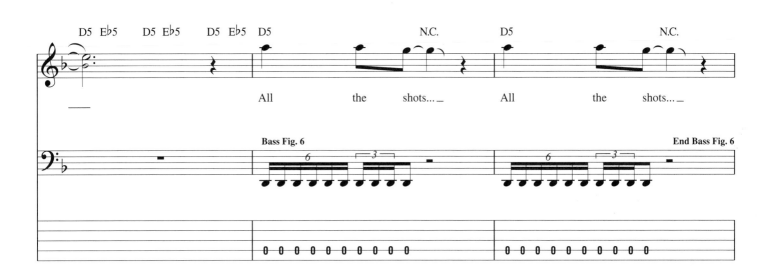

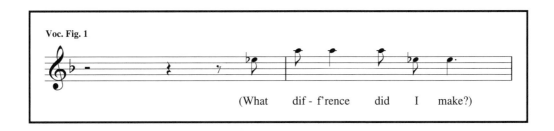

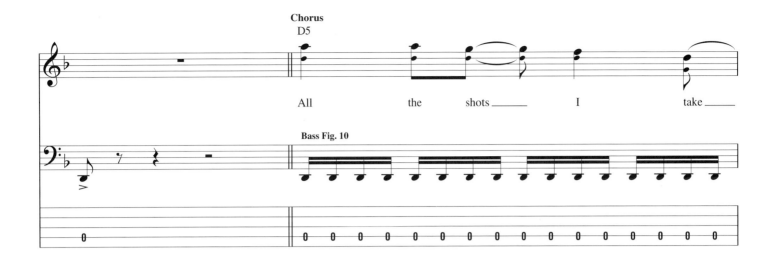

Chorus
D5

All   the   shots _____ I   take _____

Bass Fig. 10

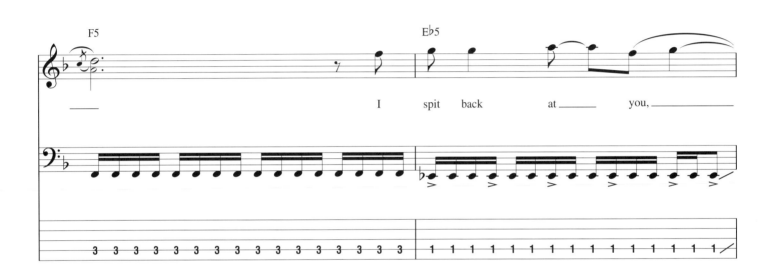

F5   **Eb5**

_____ I   spit   back   at _____ you, _____

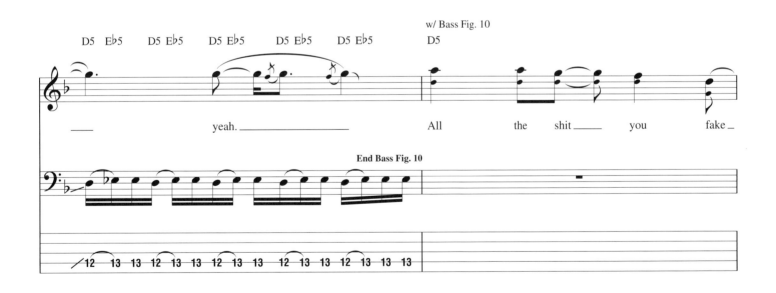

D5 Eb5   D5 Eb5   D5 Eb5   D5 Eb5   D5 Eb5   w/ Bass Fig. 10

D5

_____   yeah. _____ All   the   shit _____ you   fake _

End Bass Fig. 10

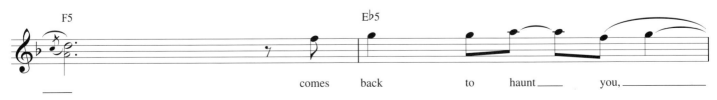

F5   **Eb5**

_____   comes   back   to   haunt _____ you, _____

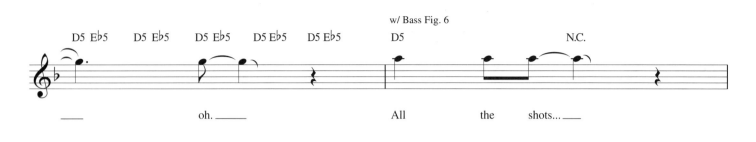

oh. _____ All the shots... _____

All the shots... _____ All the shots _____ I take _____

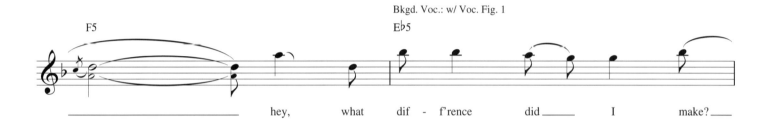

_____ hey, what dif - f'rence did _____ I make? _____

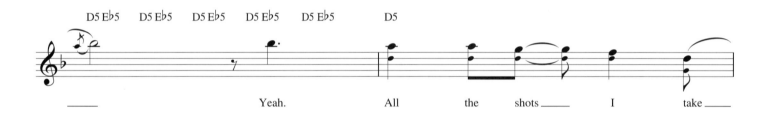

_____ Yeah. All the shots _____ I take _____

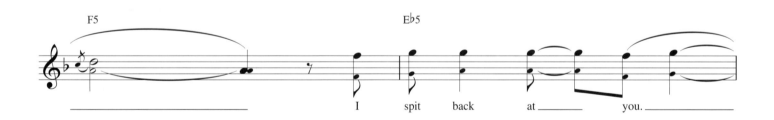

_____ I spit back at _____ you. _____

Outro

_____ Oh, _____ whoa, oh, _____ ah!

SWEET AMBER

Words and Music by
James Hetfield, Lars Ulrich,
Kirk Hammett and Bob Rock

5 str. drop D tuning, down 1 step:
(low to high) A-C-G-C-F

Intro

Moderately slow ♩ = 104

Faster ♩ = 192

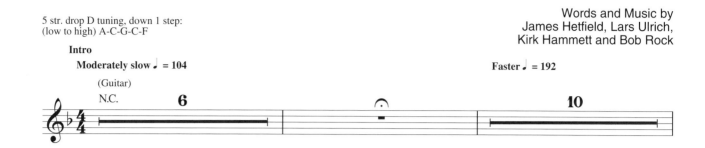

(Guitar)

Double-time feel

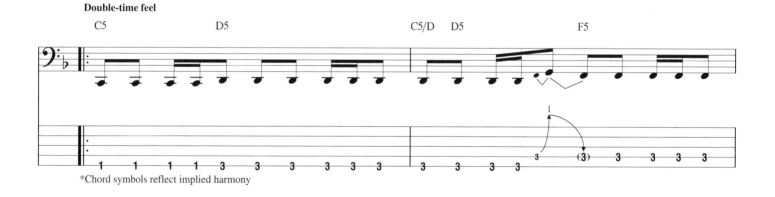

*Chord symbols reflect implied harmony

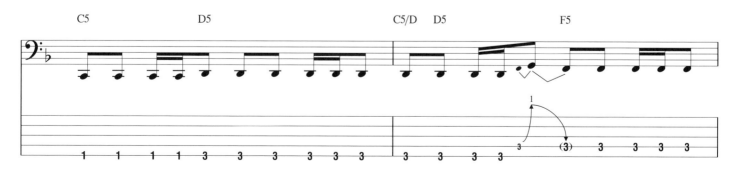

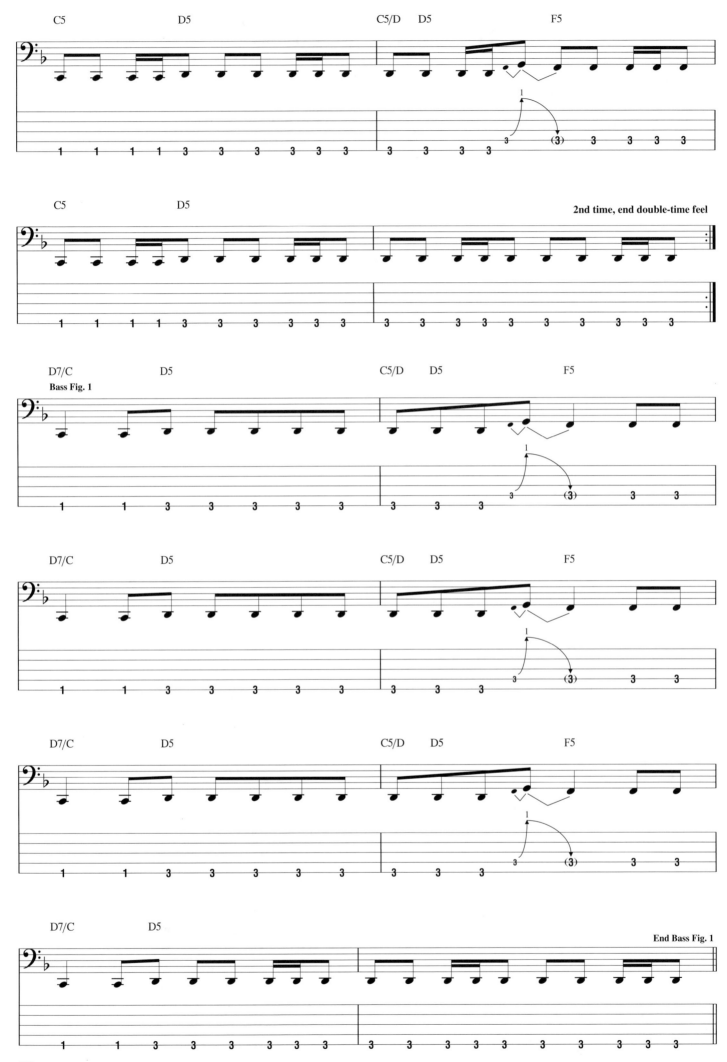

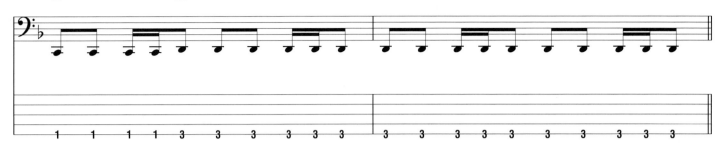

C5   D5

Coda 1

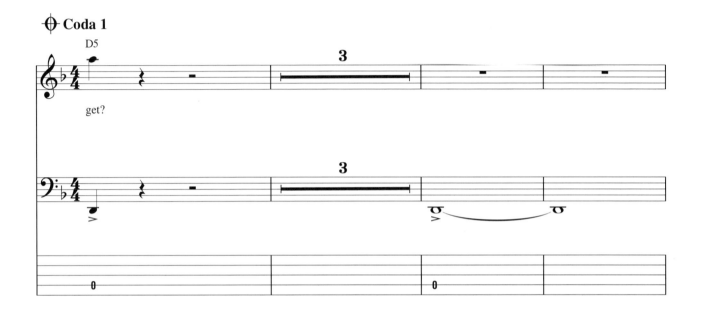

D5

get?

Interlude

Dsus2   A5   E(♭5)/B♭   A5   Dm

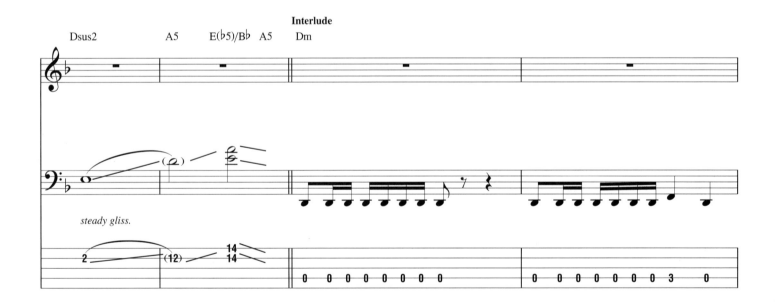

steady gliss.

Dsus2/E   A5   E(♭5)/B♭   A5   Dm

Bass Fig. 6

70

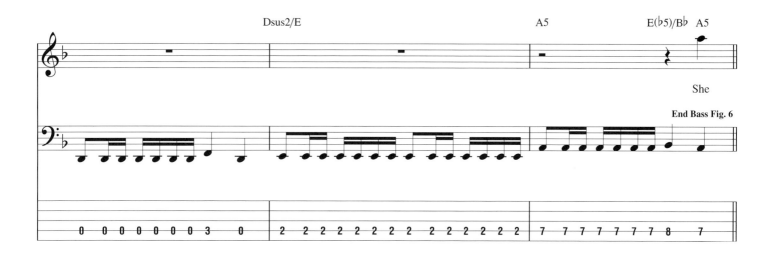

She

Bridge

w/ Bass Fig. 6 (2 times)

holds   the   pen _____   that   spells _____   the   end. _____   She   trac -

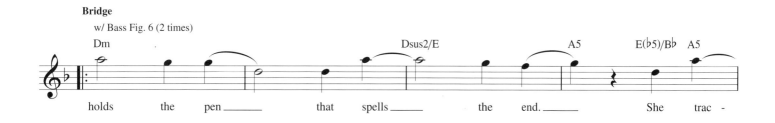

1.

- es   me _____   and   draws _____   me _____   in. _____   She

2.   w/ Bass Fig. 4

_____   Ooh, _____   sweet   am   -   ber. _____

Ooh, _____   sweet   am - ber. __

Interlude

*Chord symbols implied by gtrs.

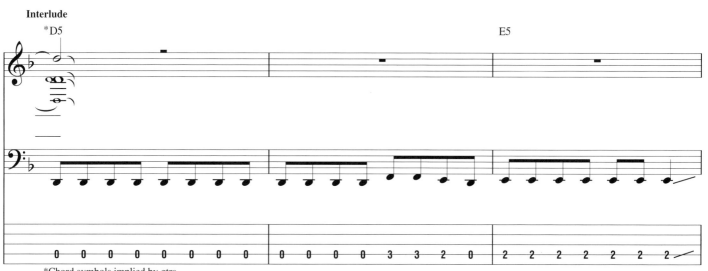

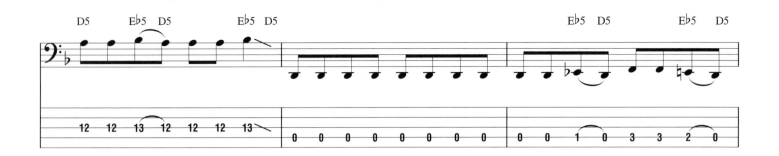

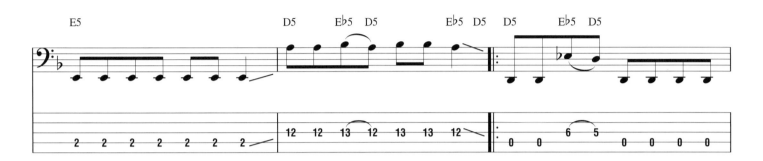

2nd time, D.S.S. al Coda 2

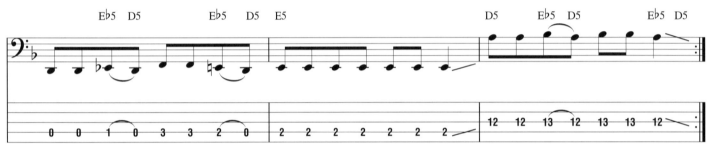

Coda 2

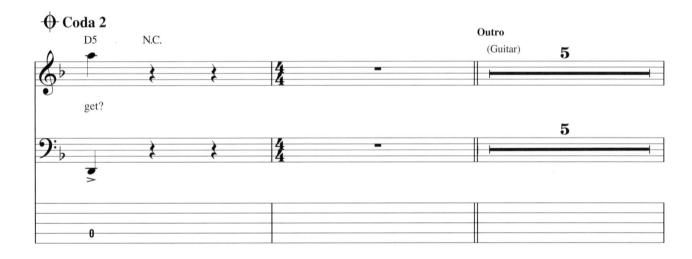

get?

Outro
(Guitar)

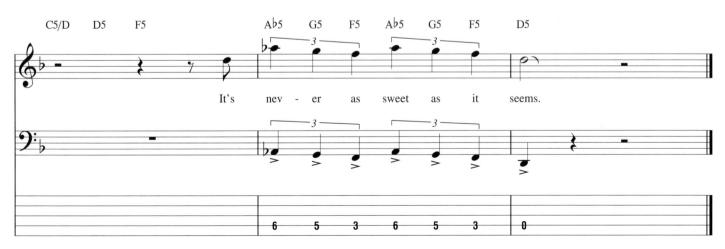

It's nev - er as sweet as it seems.

THE UNNAMED FEELING

Words and Music by
James Hetfield, Lars Ulrich,
Kirk Hammett and Bob Rock

5 str. drop D tuning, down 1 step:
(low to high) A-C-G-C-F

Moderately fast Rock ♩ = 144

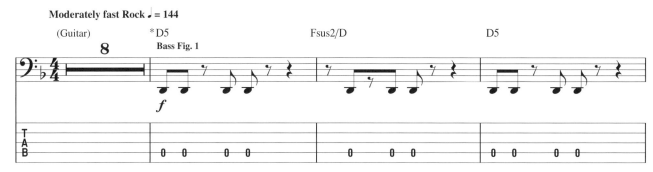

*Chord symbols reflect overall harmony.

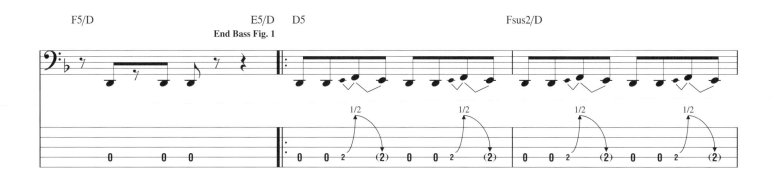

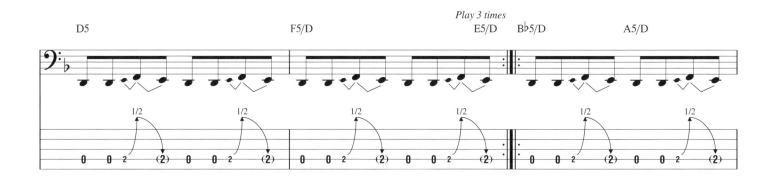

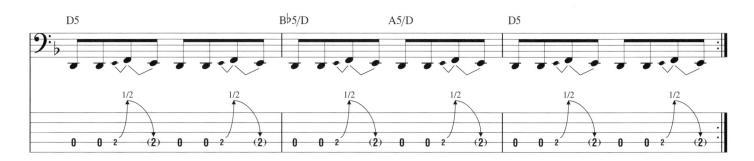

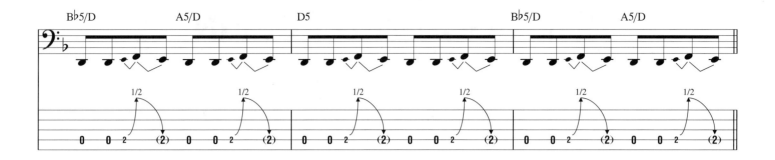

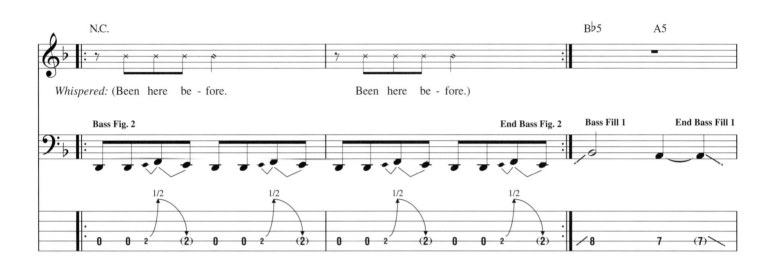

Whispered: (Been here be - fore.   Been here   be - fore.)

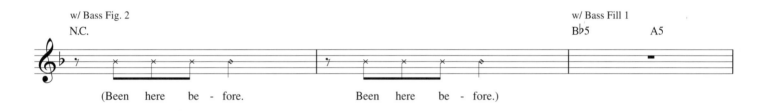

(Been here   be - fore.   Been here   be - fore.)

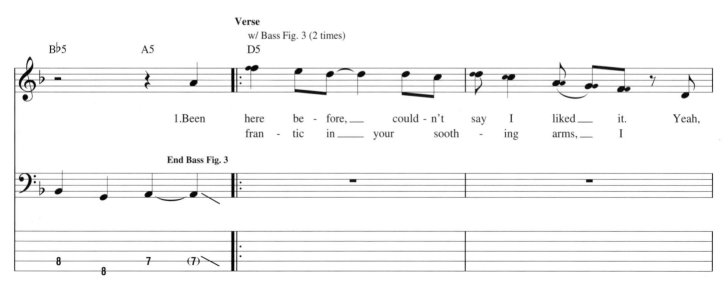

1.Been   here   be - fore,___ could - n't   say   I   liked___   it.   Yeah,
fran - tic in ___ your   sooth - ing   arms,___   I

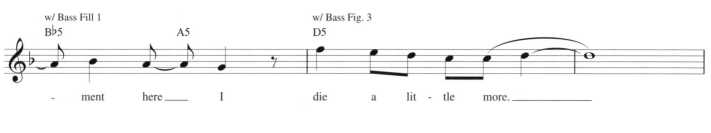

-ment here ___ I die a lit - tle more. ___

Ooh, ___ I die, ___ I die, ___ I die ___ a lit - tle more. ___

Chorus

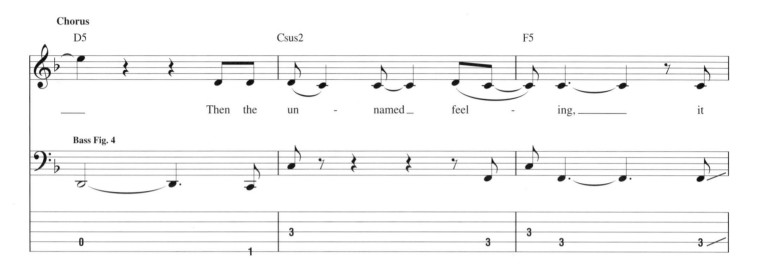

___ Then the un - named ___ feel - ing, ___ it

Bass Fig. 4

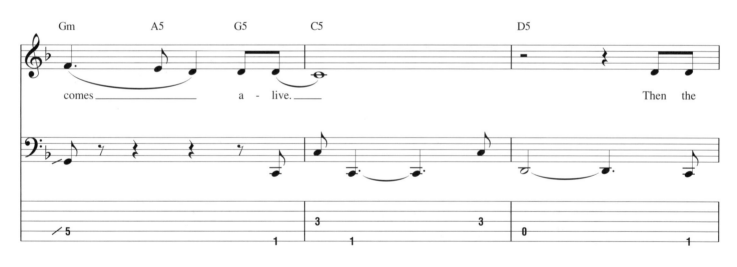

comes ___ a - live. ___ Then the

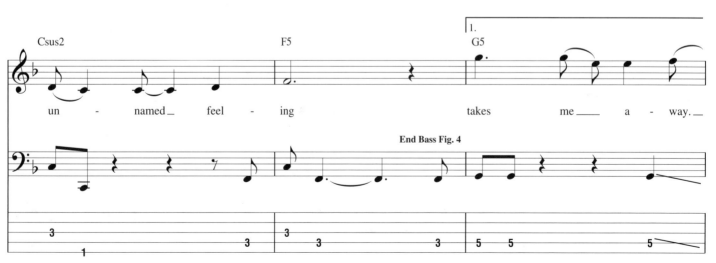

un - named ___ feel - ing takes me ___ a - way. ___

End Bass Fig. 4

w/ Bass Fig. 2 (2 times)
N.C.

Whispered: (Been here be - fore.   Been here be - fore.

Been here be - fore.   Been here be - fore.)

w/ Bass Fill 1
B♭5   A5

w/ Bass Fig. 2
N.C.

w/ Bass Fill 1
B♭5   A5

(Been here be - fore.   Been here be - fore.)

2. I'm

2.
E   F   w/ Bass Fig. 4
                      D5

treats me ___ this way. _____ And I

2   2   2   3   0

Csus2   F5/C   Gm   Gsus2   G5

wait ___ for ___ this train,   toes o - ver _____ the line. ___

C5   Csus2 C5   D5   Csus2   F5/C

_____ And then the un - named_ feel - ing, ___ it

77

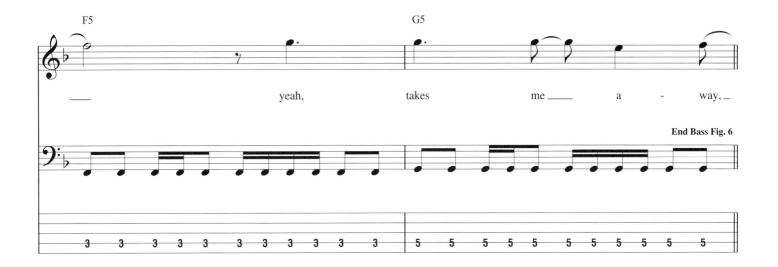

yeah, takes me a - way,

End Bass Fig. 6

Interlude
w/ Bass Fig. 1 (3 times)
N.C.

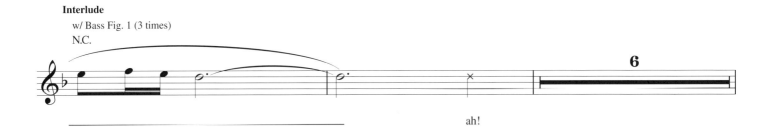

ah!

Mm, _____ uh! _____

Bridge
w/ Bass Fig. 2 (5 times)

Get the fuck ___ out of ___ here, I ___ just wan - na get ___ the fuck ___
*Chord symbols reflect overall harmony.

___ a - way ___ from ___ me. ___ I rage, ___ I glaze, ___ I hurt, ___ I hate.

___ I hate it ___ all. ___ Why? Why? ___ Why ___ me? ___ I can - not sleep ___

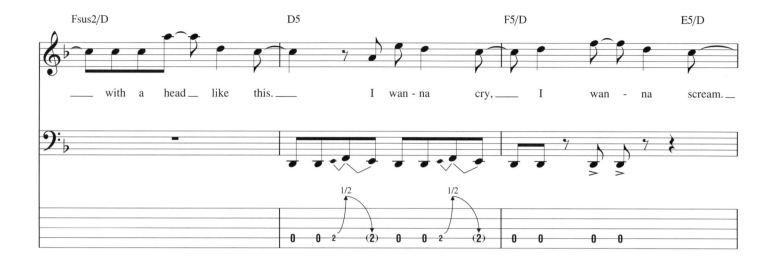

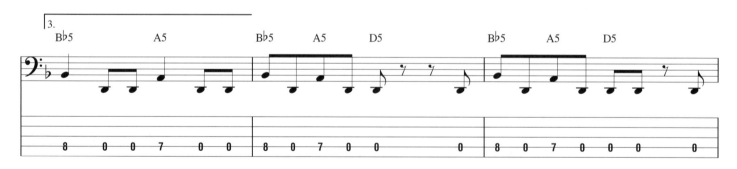

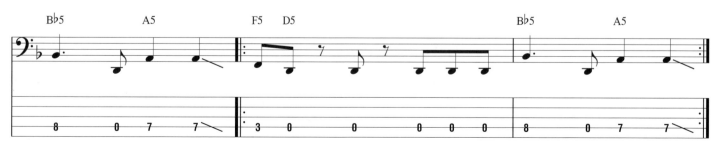

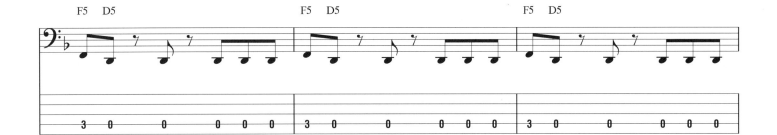

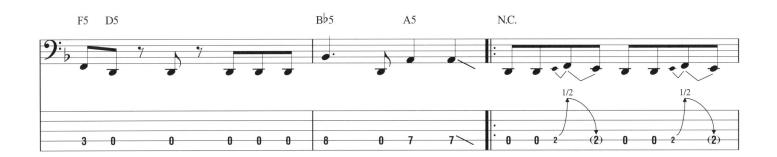

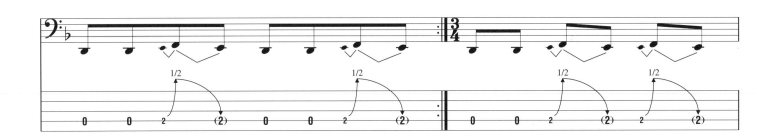

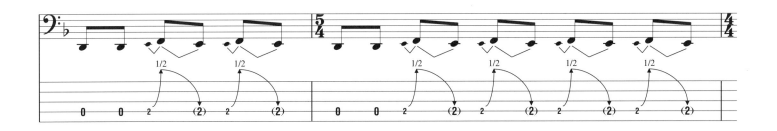

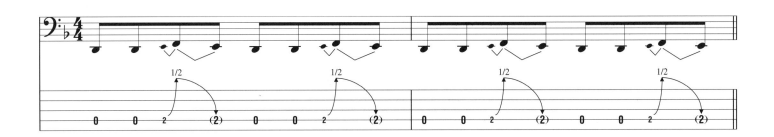

Chorus
w/ Bass Fig. 5

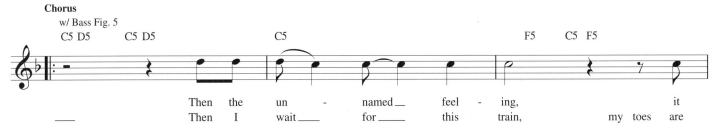

Then the un - named___ feel - ing, it
___ Then I wait___ for ___ this train, my toes are

PURIFY

Words and Music by
James Hetfield, Lars Ulrich,
Kirk Hammett and Bob Rock

5 str. drop D tuning, down 1 step:
(low to high) A-C-G-C-F

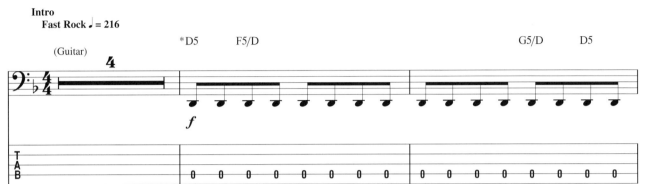

*Chord symbols reflect overall harmony,

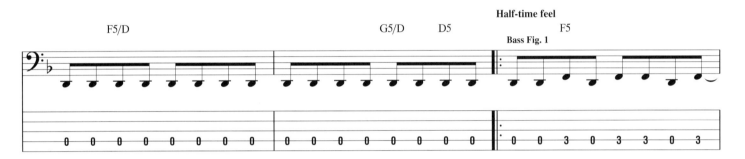

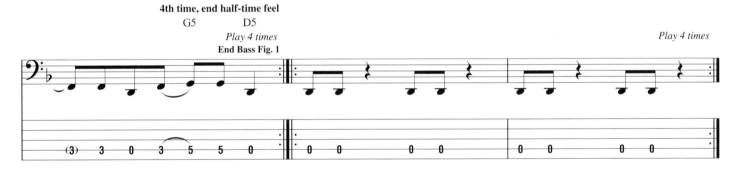

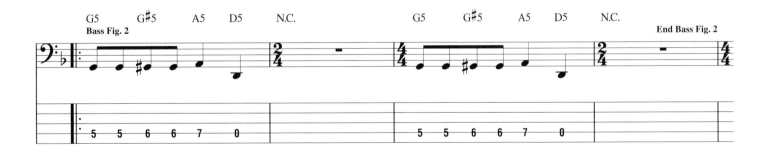

Mm, _____ ah, ha, ha, ha, ha, ha, ha!

Bridge
Half-time feel

I can find the dirt ___ on an - y - thing. _____

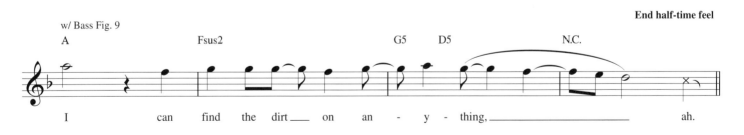

I can find the dirt ___ on an - y - thing, _____ ah.

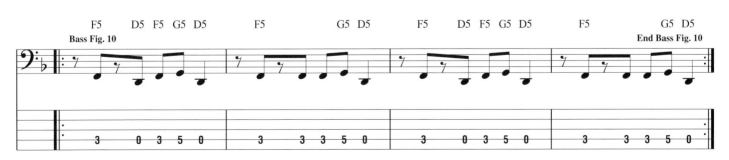

*Chord symbols reflect implied harmony.

ALL WITHIN MY HANDS

Words and Music by
James Hetfield, Lars Ulrich,
Kirk Hammett and Bob Rock

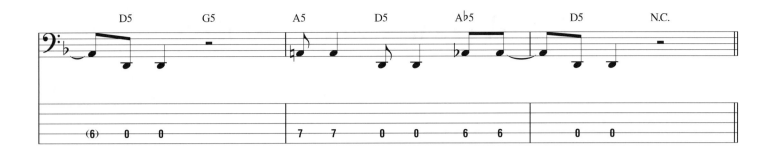

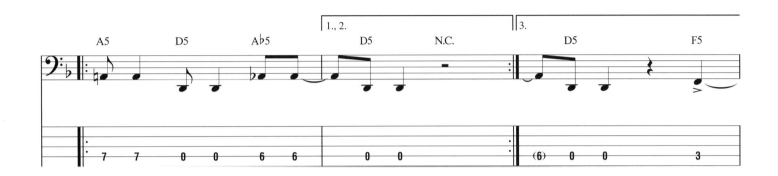

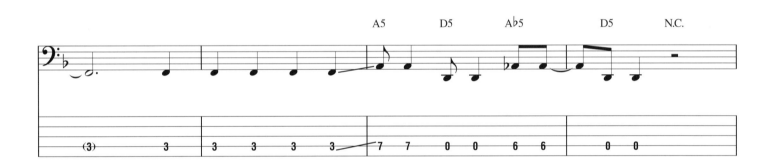

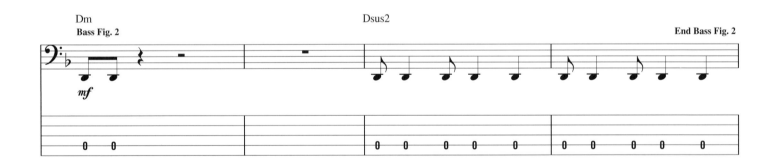

All with - in my hands. _____

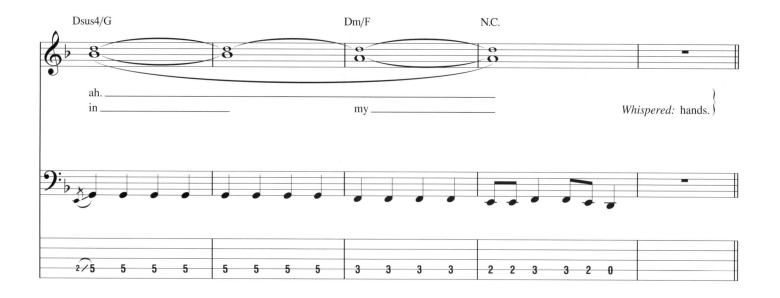

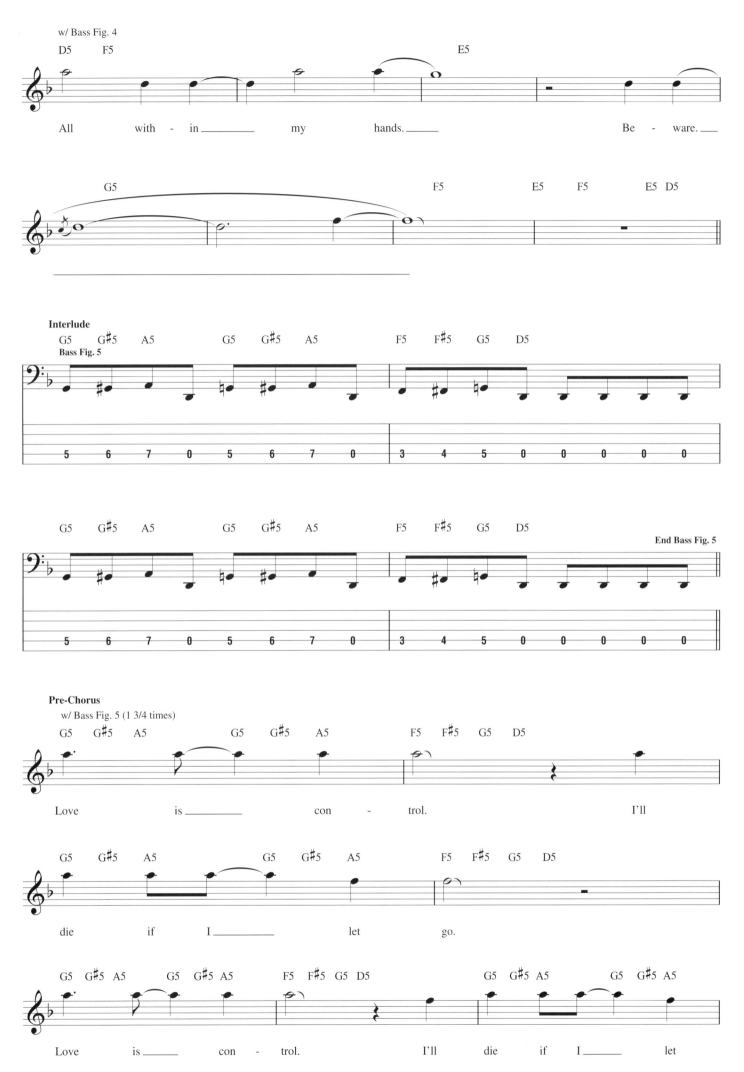

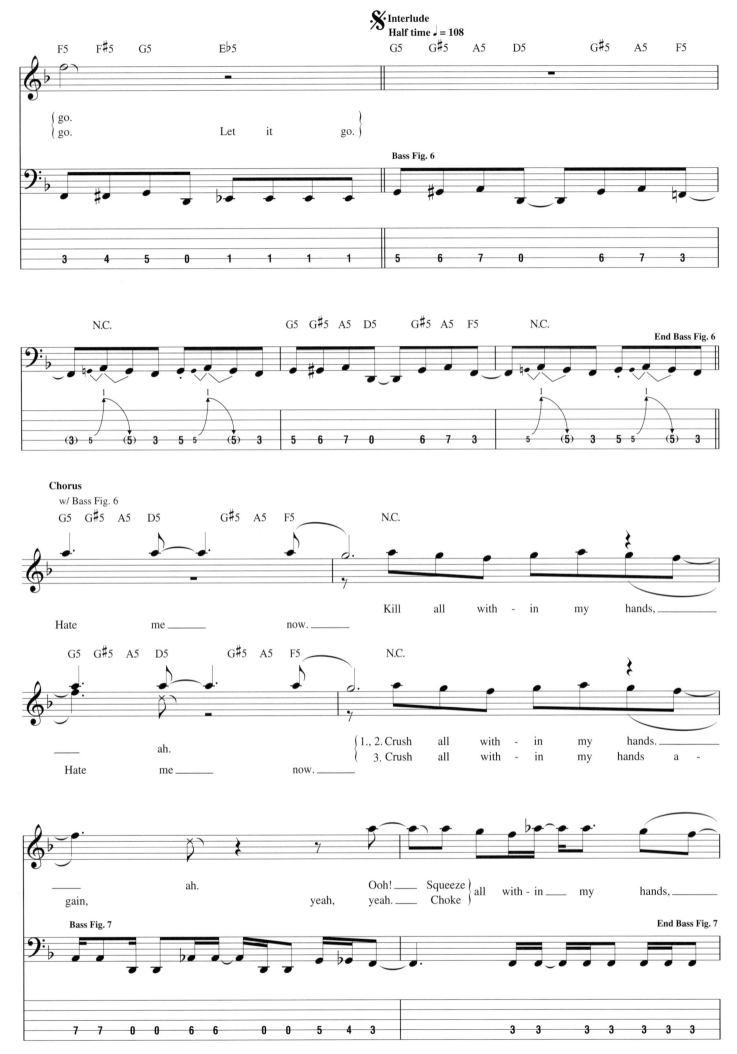

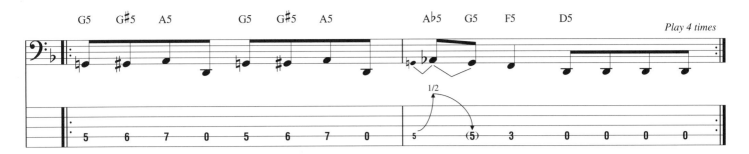

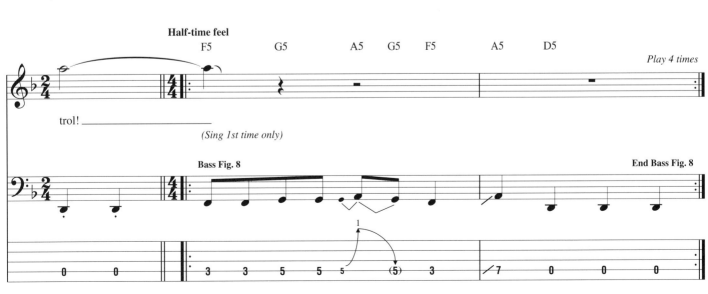

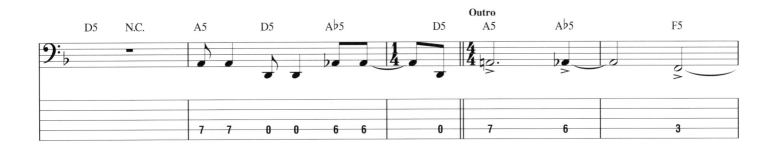

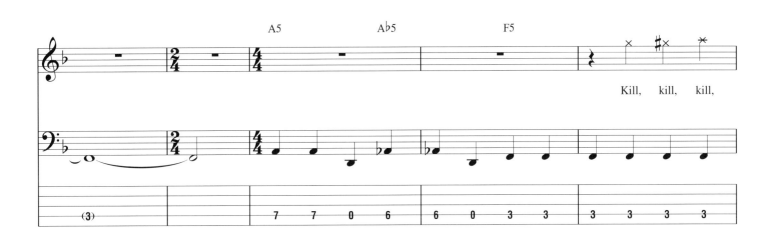

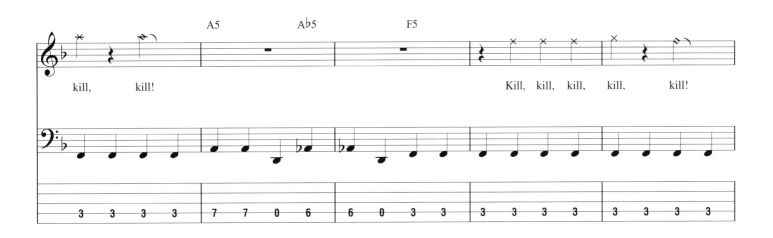

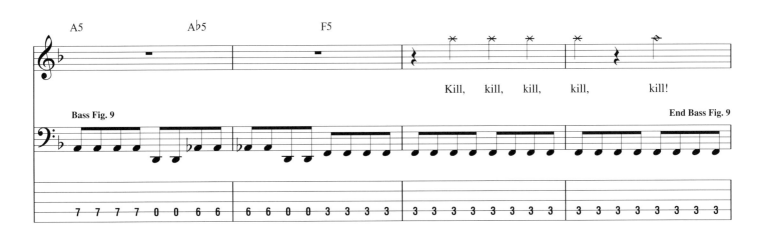

Bass Notation Legend

Bass music can be notated two different ways: on a *musical staff*, and in *tablature*.

THE MUSICAL STAFF shows pitches and rhythms and is divided by bar lines into measures. Pitches are named after the first seven letters of the alphabet.

TABLATURE graphically represents the bass fingerboard. Each horizontal line represents a string, and each number represents a fret.

Notes:

Strings:
high G
D
A
low E

3rd string, open   2nd string, 2nd fret   1st & 2nd strings open, played together

HAMMER-ON: Strike the first (lower) note with one finger, then sound the higher note (on the same string) with another finger by fretting it without picking.

PULL-OFF: Place both fingers on the notes to be sounded. Strike the first note and without picking, pull the finger off to sound the second (lower) note.

LEGATO SLIDE: Strike the first note and then slide the same fret-hand finger up or down to the second note. The second note is not struck.

SHIFT SLIDE: Same as legato slide, except the second note is struck.

TRILL: Very rapidly alternate between the notes indicated by continuously hammering on and pulling off.

TREMOLO PICKING: The note is picked as rapidly and continuously as possible.

VIBRATO: The string is vibrated by rapidly bending and releasing the note with the fretting hand.

SHAKE: Using one finger, rapidly alternate between two notes on one string by sliding either a half-step above or below.

NATURAL HARMONIC: Strike the note while the fret hand lightly touches the string directly over the fret indicated.

MUFFLED STRINGS: A percussive sound is produced by laying the fret hand across the string(s) without depressing them and striking them with the pick hand.

BEND: Strike the note and bend up the interval shown.

BEND AND RELEASE: Strike the note and bend up as indicated, then release back to the original note. Only the first note is struck.

RIGHT-HAND TAP: Hammer ("tap") the fret indicated with the "pick-hand" index or middle finger and pull off to the note fretted by the fret hand.

LEFT-HAND TAP: Hammer ("tap") the fret indicated with the "fret-hand" index or middle finger.

SLAP: Strike ("slap") string with right-hand thumb.

POP: Snap ("pop") string with right-hand index or middle finger.

Additional Musical Definitions

(accent)	•	Accentuate note (play it louder)
(accent)	•	Accentuate note with great intensity
(staccato)	•	Play the note short
⊓	•	Downstroke
⋁	•	Upstroke
D.S. al Coda	•	Go back to the sign (𝄋), then play until the measure marked "*To Coda*," then skip to the section labelled "**Coda**."

D.C. al Fine	•	Go back to the beginning of the song and play until the measure marked "*Fine*" (end).
Bass Fig.	•	Label used to recall a recurring pattern.
Fill	•	Label used to identify a brief pattern which is to be inserted into the arrangement.
tacet	•	Instrument is silent (drops out).
	•	Repeat measures between signs.
1. 2.	•	When a repeated section has different endings, play the first ending only the first time and the second ending only the second time.

NOTE: Tablature numbers in parentheses mean:
1. The note is being sustained over a system (note in standard notation is tied), or
2. The note is sustained, but a new articulation (such as a hammer-on, pull-off, slide or vibrato begins), or
3. The note is a barely audible "ghost" note (note in standard notation is also in parentheses).